Successful Stress Management

The Guide to Manage Stress, Deal with Changes,
Relieve Anxiety, Work Success and Live Happily

Minnie Davidson

© **Copyright 2020 - All rights reserved.**

The content contained within this book may not be reproduced, duplicated or transmitted without direct written permission from the author or the publisher.

Under no circumstances will any blame or legal responsibility be held against the publisher, or author, for any damages, reparation, or monetary loss due to the information contained within this book, either directly or indirectly.

Legal Notice:

This book is copyright protected. It is only for personal use. You cannot amend, distribute, sell, use, quote or paraphrase any part, or the content within this book, without the consent of the author or publisher.

Disclaimer Notice:

Please note the information contained within this document is for educational and entertainment purposes only. All effort has been executed to present accurate, up to date, reliable, complete information. No warranties of any kind are declared or implied. Readers acknowledge that the author is not engaging in the rendering of legal, financial, medical or professional advice. The content within this book has been derived from various sources. Please consult a licensed professional before attempting any techniques outlined in this book.

By reading this document, the reader agrees that under no circumstances is the author responsible for any losses, direct or indirect, that are incurred as a result of the use of information contained within this document, including, but not limited to, errors, omissions, or inaccuracies.

TABLE OF CONTENTS

Introduction 7

    Chapter 1: Understanding Stress 13

    Chapter 2 : The Two Extremes of Stress 27

    Chapter 3 : Learning to Remain Calm and be in Control 47

    Chapter 4 : Dealing with Workplace Stress .. 61

    Chapter 5 : How to Control Stress in Life 83

    Chapter 6 : Minimalist Lifestyle Tips to Help Control Stress 97

    Chapter 7 : How to Successfully Deal with Changes and Challenges in Life and at Work 111

    Chapter 8 : Learning to Manage Your Worries and Anxiety 119

    Chapter 9 : Drawing the Line to Separate Your Home from Work 135

    Chapter 10 : Tips to Enable You Live a Happier Life 149

Conclusion 167

References 171

INTRODUCTION

Relating to your family and going to work can affect your interpersonal relationships. This is often due to the possibility of stress creeping into your life. We all go through stressful situations, but what makes us different is how we handle them.

If you fall into the category of individuals who let their stress take center stage, then you're inevitably going to notice the effects in your daily life. Your problem lies in your inability to manage and overcome stress in your life properly. So, how do you get your life back in order?

This book holds information that will provide solutions to your problem. Everything that is essential in achieving your goal of dealing with stress both at your home and at work is all present herein. If you aren't sure what is causing your stress, then you will learn about the various stress-inducing situations and also how you may be introducing stress through your anger and worries.

There is also a look at the various types of stress you may be experiencing, including the positive aspects of stress. Yes, stress can have benefits in your life. It all depends on how well you understand it. All these will offer a guide in overcoming this issue in your life.

Although there are bound to be significant differences in our lives, stress is one area where we humans often have similar experiences. The situations that induce this stress and how we will handle it may not differ. This is what makes it so easy for me to help others dealing with the same problem.

I have been in that position, and I understand your experiences. To make it easier to identify with me, simply consider me as the person beside you in a support group. The one who has overcome stress and a part of the support group to help others achieve the same result.

During the period I was struggling with stress, there were so many things I was doing wrong. I think my biggest issue was my inability to reach out for help. I didn't read books on stress management, connect with others, or seek medical advice.

Although this book isn't a substitute for medical advice, it is a culmination of my experiences. These are the various steps I took in overcoming stress in my life. These are experiences that you will be able to relate with in your everyday activities.

I understand how easy it is to go through life letting your stress and worries drag you down. I want this writing to be a way to help you cut yourself off from these burdens and begin to move on in life.

While I want you to be armed after reading this book, it won't make you dangerous. What you get is the right information that you can use as tools in solving your problem. You will get yourself out of that downward spiral and learn to live a stress-free life.

Do you understand what a stress-free life will look like for you? This may be difficult for you to imagine at this point, so I will give you something to picture. Just imagine how a young baby goes through life.

They sleep peacefully and are always happy. This is what you can expect of life after reading this book. You will be filled with positivity and adopt the right approach in handling the various situations that you might experience in life.

I know a lot of people, friends, and family who are much happier in their approach toward life. This wasn't always the case for these individuals. What better way to find out how useful the information you provide is than through its effects on those around you?

This is the same approach I took in assessing how useful this book will be in the life of others. I put it to good use in improving the lives of those around me. Not only was this beneficial in their lives, it also had a positive impact on my life.

In overcoming their stress, it also reduced the burden on me. Now I don't have to worry about anyone spreading their negativity. I was also able to prevent any future occurrence of my partner coming home irritated and frustrated. This was the point of a positive turnaround in my relationship.

This information is what you will get in this book. Your success, however, depends on how you apply this information I offer. Are you going to take an immediate step? Or will you procrastinate until the stress becomes unbearable?

With the help I offer through this book, I believe you will take the right step. I'm confident that you will become more knowledgeable about stress and stress management. You will become a walking expert in handling this situation.

If you've taken the step to get this book, I'm sure you're not going to procrastinate. You need to take immediate action. If you keep procrastinating, then the right day may never come.

People who achieve success don't wait around for the right things to happen; they make it happen. Use this book as your guide in making the right things happen in your life today.

As you read this book, you find that each chapter has the essential information you need to get a step closer to what you want. In addition to understanding stress better, you also get practical information that you can apply to change your life. I put in all the details, and there is nothing hidden from you.

Do you ever wonder how your anger might be affecting you? How your work is pulling down the relationships you have built? How is it affecting your health? Or how you are interfering with the lives of others due to stress in your life?

Start your journey toward answering these questions by reading this book today.

CHAPTER 1:
UNDERSTANDING STRESS

What is Stress?

As humans, a part of our daily life consists of us going through changes. To keep up with these changes, the body must react appropriately. Stress refers to how the body responds to these changes.

It is a means by which the body prepares you for a new situation. This can be emotionally, physically, or mentally. An individual will choose either a fight or flight response in such circumstances.

The stress we experience can either be positive or negative. When stress is positive, then it comes to motivate you, alert, and prepare you for impending danger so you can avoid it. Negative stress usually occurs when there are too many stressors.

The presence of excess stressors will result in tension and overwork due to stress. This is due to the inability of the body to get any form of rest before the next stressful situation. It can result in distress, which is your reaction to negative stress.

What are Stressors?

Stressors refer to the various situations or events that your body interprets as a threat. These serve as a trigger to the stress response mechanism of the body. In simpler form, they are events that promote stress in your life.

How Does Pressure Influence Stress?

One of the simplest things that you notice from your interaction with other individuals is the fact that you are different in so many ways. These include your speech patterns, hair color, weight, tics, and reactions to similar situations. The same applies when discussing stress.

In this discussion, it is common to bring up the issue of pressure. This is often one of the reasons why some people find themselves experiencing stress. Nonetheless, not everyone will feel the same way.

Pressure for some individuals provides motivation, stimulation, and a drive to complete a task. For another individual, this same level of pressure might produce a higher level of stress hormones in the body. This is where our unique differences play a role.

What this implies is that what you may find to be the optimum level of pressure you need to work effectively and creatively will lead to stress in the life of another person. This can be in the form of burnout or anxiety. There is also an issue when you are getting below the optimum level of pressure.

This lack of optimum pressure can lead to a situation in which you are depressed, bored, or apathetic. There is a possibility of reaching 'rustout' due to this lack of pressure. Rustout refers to a situation in which you're unable to reach your full potential due to a lack of challenge.

Understanding these two unique situations, burnout, and rustout, it is much easier to differentiate pressure from stress. While pressure can lead to both rustout and burnout, it only results in stress if it is tilting toward the burnout level.

Balancing the level of pressure to suit your optimum level is essential if you want to avoid stress and also prevent the frustration, depression, boredom, or apathy that is present when you're not getting enough challenge.

Types of Stress

There are various types of stress that you can experience. To a large extent, the effect of stress on your body depends on the type you are experiencing. These are some of the kinds of stress that you can experience:

Chronic Stress

Chronic stress refers to any form of stress that an individual experience continuously for long periods. If you are experiencing any form of stress that you feel is impossible to escape, then this might be a sign of chronic stress. In several cases, when you fail to resolve acute stress, it can develop into chronic stress.

There are various examples of chronic stress, including an unhealthy marriage, trauma, financial difficulties, an inconvenient job, and so on. Considering the numerous health issues attributed to stress, chronic stress is a crucial contributor to some of these health issues, including:

- Cirrhosis of the liver

- Heart diseases
- Accidents
- Suicide
- Cancer
- Lung diseases

Eustress

This is any form of stress that you experience that provides excitement, fun, or benefit to you. Moments when you experience an increase in adrenaline levels are usually closely related to eustress. An example of such moments is when you are exercising.

Acute Stress

Anytime you experience stress that lasts only a short time is usually acute stress. Both positive and negative stress can fall into the category of acute stress. When this form of stress occurs at different times, it can provide some benefits to the body.

Situations that promote acute stress usually trigger the fight-or-flight mechanism of the body. This is how the body appropriately responds to any new demand, challenge, or event. Following these situations, the body can develop on the best and most effective response to such cases if it occurs in the future.

A common example of positive acute stress includes getting on a rollercoaster. Negative acute stress can be experienced in situations such as arguments with your spouse or a near-miss accident. Depending on the severity of the acute stress, there may be lasting health issues.

An example of this is noticeable in individuals with post-traumatic stress disorder. These individuals develop this disorder as a result of experiencing a life-threatening situation or a crime.

Episodic Acute Stress

In typical situations, acute stress should be short-term and infrequent. Regardless, there are situations when it becomes regular and a part of the daily life of an individual. In such cases, it becomes episodic acute stress.

These individuals have come to the conclusion that there is a need for stress in their daily life. Due to this acceptance, changing to a healthier lifestyle is difficult. This form of stress is common in individuals who exhibit anxiety, irritability, and a short temper.

This chaotic lifestyle is also noticeable in pessimistic individuals who are always looking for the negative in every situation.

Health Issues Due to Stress

Your health is your priority when dealing with stress. It may seem insignificant when considering it over a short-term, but long-term exposure to stress will take its toll on your body. There are different ways that this can happen.

Here are some of the common health issues that are associated with stressful situations:

Accelerated Aging

Accelerated aging has always been an issue in discussions regarding stress. To provide facts regarding this issue, there have been various studies and research. There are several ways through which stress can cause accelerated aging in individuals (Gregoire, 2013):

Damage to Cells

This is due to workplace stress in our lives. By measuring the telomeres of different individuals, a study was able to determine that those with higher workplace stress levels had shorter telomere. The adverse effects associated with the shortening of the telomeres include cardiovascular diseases, Parkinson's, cancer, and type 2 diabetes.

It Ages the Brain

In another study by UC Berkeley, scientists identified that in females, higher stress levels could promote a rapid brain decline, which is aging-related.

Unhealthy Lifestyle Choices

Your habits have an effect on proper aging. Poor habits like sleep deprivation is a result of stress in your life. Sleep deprivation is one of the factors that promote rapid aging.

It is also common to ignore exercises and don't eat a balanced diet while under stress. These individuals rely more on medications and alcohol. This will surely become noticeable in how the body ages.

It Results in Loss of Vision and Hearing

Another result from research shows that due to the continuous production of adrenaline over time, there is a noticeable constriction of the blood vessels. This constriction can cause a drop in vision and hearing of the individual.

More research is necessary to determine if this decrease is permanent, so we can assume that a temporary hearing and vision loss is possible due to stress.

Diabetes

Diabetes is another health issue that is affected and promoted by stress. In the people suffering from type 1 or type 2 diabetes, they suffer from the effects of physical stress. This form of stress causes a rise in the blood sugar level of the individual.

With mental stress, it might affect individuals with type 1 diabetes differently. For some, there will be an increase in blood glucose levels, while others will experience a decrease. For those with type 2 diabetes, there is also an issue when they are under mental stress. This type of stress results in a rise in the blood glucose level of the individual.

Stress can also promote diabetes. This is noticeable in the increase in the chances of an individual adopting bad behavior. In this case, unhealthy food choices.

They resort to excessive drinking and eating a poor diet. This might also affect those already suffering from this condition.

Depression

Depression is one of the health issues that can result from chronic or acute stress. This situation occurs when the body is unable to shut-down and reset the stress response system after overcoming a stressful situation. A tasking job that offers minimal rewards or the loss of a loved one is one of such events.

Such events result in the reduction of neurotransmitters such as dopamine and serotonin, with an increase in cortisol levels. Due to the inability to shut-down the stress response, the body is unable to return these levels to normal, meaning that the body will be unable to function optimally.

This means there will be a dopamine deficiency in the body, which has a close link to depression in humans (Cadman & Falck, 2018). With lower stress levels, the risk of depression is much lower.

Obesity

Another significant health problem that individuals may experience due to stress is obesity. There have been research with conclusions that prove this to be a fact. In one study, the samples used in determining this risk was the hair cortisol level (Whiteman, 2017).

According to this study, individuals with a higher hair cortisol level also had a heavier weight, bigger waist circumference, and higher body mass index (BMI). In comparison to excess fat in the hips and leg area, excess belly fat poses a more significant health risk.

There is also the issue of "comfort eating," in which individuals try to make themselves feel better by consuming foods that have high sugar and fat content. This is an action that also promotes obesity, and this "comfort eating" is a result of stress.

Premature Death

If you don't manage stress properly, there is a high risk that it can shorten your lifespan. This includes the everyday stress you experience in life. Through chronic stress, there is a possibility of an increase in blood pressure.

This form of stress also reduces your immunity and affects your memory due to the rise in the level of cortisol in the body. In other situations, your reaction to everyday stress also has a role to play.

Heart Diseases

To establish a direct link between stress and heart diseases, there is a need for in-depth research into this area. Nonetheless, there are other indirect ways by which stress can lead to heart diseases.

There is a possibility of stress leading to heart muscle inflammation. This is one of the areas that play a role in heart diseases. The possibility of causing a sudden jump in your blood pressure is also present with stress.

People who experience stress tend to overeat, smoke, and drink. This is their solution to get over stress, but these actions also increase the risk of heart disease. There is also a risk of heart attack, hypertension, or stroke due to the damage to the blood vessel lining of an individual experiencing chronic stress.

How These Health Issues Adversely Affect Your Family

When you are down with health issues due to stress, you can expect it to have an unwanted effect on your family members. The first comes in need to care for you. The things you could do on your own may no longer be possible.

As a result, you need the assistance of others. This means if the family can't afford a nurse to be by your side at all times, then someone has to be around you.

Another way is the financial setback it causes, no one will be blaming you for your predicament, but the strain on the family finances will show. In addition to spending on treatment, you might not have the opportunity to work as you could before. Not everyone gets to perform at their peak despite battling a health issue.

It is also vital that you note that illnesses will cause a lifestyle change in your family. How it affects each family member will differ. Regardless of how it affects them, there are going to be some changes that they must accept.

CHAPTER 2 : THE TWO EXTREMES OF STRESS

What are the Two Extremes of Stress?

In dealing with stress, there are two extremes that you must consider. These are the stress-inducing extreme and the stress control extreme. This is essential since there is a solution to the stress you are currently facing.

The stress-inducing extreme refers to the events that create stress in your life. These are everyday situations that I will discuss in this chapter. Activities that are within the stress-inducing extreme include the following:

- Moving to a new house
- Getting into financial troubles
- Going through a divorce

The other extreme is the stress control extreme. This encompasses the different steps you can take in minimizing and eliminating the stress you experience from a situation. These control measures may differ when tackling your work-related stress.

The stress control extreme also covers the various methods that you can use to prevent work-related stress from getting into your home. In this chapter, we will focus on the stress-inducing extreme. I will explain to you the way these situations can induce stress in your life.

Everyday Situations That Induce Stress in Life

Identifying the situations that induce stress on a daily basis is essential in dealing with stress. These are the events that you must go through every day or at least once in your lifetime, such as getting stuck in traffic. Here are some others that you will easily relate to:

Getting into a Fight with Loved Ones or Friends

The fight I refer to in this case is a heated argument that you get into with another person. This is when this argument causes you to say things that you can't take back, leading to the end of the relationship. This is a stressful event in your life.

After the fight, you usually have lingering feelings of upset and anger, coupled with the fact that you just cut off communication with someone close to you. This person was once a confidant or companion, and this loss will create a hole in your heart.

Going Through a Divorce

A divorce is one of the significant events that creates stress in our lives. This stress remains present even if there is a mutual agreement between the partners. While you may feel happy to be free from your former partner finally, there are downsides to this process.

These are due to some of the steps that you must take to complete the divorce. Some of these steps include court proceedings, dealing with the issue of child custody, making financial arrangements, and also living arrangements. These are some of the processes that make divorce very stressful.

This process also has adverse effects on your kids. It is easy to overlook this area when struggling to get a divorce since your main concern is often about your emotional and mental well-being. To a young child, the separation of their parents is misinterpreted as being due to something they might have done.

The inability of children to adequately express their emotions makes it more difficult for them. Despite these adverse effects, there are periods when a divorce is the only option. These are cases where you must come up with effective ways of dealing with stress.

You can start by ensuring that there is an excellent support system in place. This support system isn't only for your benefit, but it is also beneficial to the well-being of your children. In reducing the stress that your children go through, it is crucial to remain in contact with your former partner—no fighting or arguments around the children.

Keeping yourself fit by remaining active physically can assist in overcoming the mental and emotional stress you experience. Lastly, it is essential to take time to think about any decision you decide to take. The emotional turmoil that you experience during a divorce can interfere with your ability to make the right decisions.

Marriage

While going through a divorce may seem like something that may never happen in your life, you can expect marriage to happen sometime in the future. This is for anyone who is still enjoying the single life. There are a lot of things that change when you decide to get married.

Forget about the euphoria that is supposed to come with a wedding; there are other things that you must consider. The wedding planning is one of the things that creates a lot of stress. You have to get a venue, send out your invites, and get your wedding dress or suit prepared.

There is also the issue of conflicts in the family. How will you get everyone to cooperate? What do you need to put in place to ensure that everyone has a great time during the wedding?

Establishing good communication is an excellent step to take if you want to have a successful wedding. Let everyone know what your plans are and how you want the wedding to go. The next issue comes after the wedding.

This is when you have to start adjusting to living with your partner. For some people, they already have an idea of how things will be following their experience while dating. Not everyone gets to have this opportunity. Some of the things you experience during the marriage will still come as a surprise.

One of the issues during the early periods of my marriage was due to finances. While I was good at following a budget, I always had problems getting my partner to do the same. This was my primary stressor at the time.

Getting past this issue took time and excellent communication. In a marriage, communication is key. Let your partner know what is killing you inside. This will provide the opportunity for both parties to work toward a lasting solution.

Financial Setbacks

Another common life event that causes stress is financial setbacks. No money to pay your bills, inability to pay for your kids' tuition, and many more issues that come with a lack of money can hurt you. They lead to excessive worrying about how you will resolve the situation.

There are several reasons why you may find yourself experiencing financial setbacks. A poor investment decision can play a huge role in financial setbacks. When you decide to invest your money in a company without doing proper research, you can end up losing all your investment.

Another reason is your poor spending habits. Are you continually giving in to your impulses? Are you buying things you don't need? These are everyday spending habits that put you in an awkward position financially.

If you are frequently changing your cars or moving from a smaller house to a bigger house, it might also be a problem. This is a serious issue if you're taking out loans for these purchases. Overdependence on credit cards can also play a role in financial setbacks.

There are some steps you can take to prevent yourself from falling into financial situations that cause stress. These include the following:

Identifying Your Stressor

Everyone has a stressor that may not apply to other individuals. Identifying this stressor is the first step to overcoming their financial woes. For some individuals, they may often have monthly expenses that are higher than their monthly income.

For others, they have spending habits that cause them to max out their credit cards. To identify your unique trait that is leading to these issues, then you should observe your spending from the perspective of an outsider.

Once you can identify these causes, you need to create a plan to help you overcome them. If you are giving in to impulse purchases, then limit the amount of money on you when going shopping. If your problem is with your use of credit cards, then switch to a cash-only system.

Seek Help if Necessary

The belief that you can solve your problems without the help of others is often the reason why you may find yourself neck-deep in stressful situations. Learn to rely on others to overcome your financial challenges. You likely have a lot of friends that know more about how to handle money than you do.

You can also turn to the experts for advice. In some companies, there are financial wellness programs in place to assist employees. If your company offers one such program, then don't feel ashamed to sign up. Thinking of what others will say doesn't provide a solution to your underlying problem. You will lose a lot of friends if they begin to tag you as a financial liability.

Debt management, budgeting, and healthy spending habits are some critical areas where an expert can assist you.

Look for Opportunities to Earn More

An extra income can lessen the burden and stress of your financial setbacks. If you have a lot of time on your hands, then look for any additional jobs you can take to make ends meet. Developing multiple streams of income also helps.

In developing multiple streams of income, it will only be possible if you have attained financial stability. Be sure to perform extensive research before beginning this process. This is to ensure you don't fall back into financial issues.

As you will learn later on, minimalism can help when it comes to making extra income. Scour your home for items that you no longer need. Put them on sale and profit from them. That other car or spare TV that you no longer need can fetch you a decent amount of money.

Being Out of a Job

A job is often one of the most important things to have when you reach adulthood. This is unless you become an entrepreneur, which enables you to be your boss. You need a job to make money, and a career is often a passion that motivates a lot of people.

Losing your job and having to sit at home can lead to stress, depression, and humiliation. The stress appears when you have to worry about how to make ends meet consistently. It is also an issue when you have to make a lifestyle change.

Getting fired is a direct attack on your self-esteem. This is in addition to the fact that it forces you to learn how to get by on less money. Your situation might be better than others if you were smart enough to build up your savings while working.

Unless you can quickly adjust to this new lifestyle, then there is no way to overcome this stress. Another option is to get a new job, and this may not happen as fast as you want it. This can add to your stressor as you begin to think that you aren't good enough.

While this is understandable, it is also possible to experience stress when starting a new job. This includes quitting your old job for a better one. How is something that is supposed to be good a stressor?

The reason is that a new job can become overwhelming. Knowing what your role at this new environment is and developing a new routine has its side effects. You are untested in this new place, so you're under the impression that you have to make a positive impact.

To ease the stress in this situation, the first step is to slow down and ask questions. Interacting with others can help you get a better handle of what is expected of you. No one expects you to fully grasp the operations of the company on your first day.

What they expect is that you should communicate with others when you need help. This is much better than trying to do it all on your own and making mistakes.

Health Challenges

Another common stressor in life is in the form of health challenges. This is one that has a significant impact on you and other members of the family. Everyone has to create time to ensure that they are there for you. This can be physically, emotionally, and financially.

You don't have to be in the hospital to experience health challenges. This is what makes it difficult for individuals. You might be struggling with stress in other areas of your life while battling the pain and stress that comes with your health challenges.

The financial burden of dealing with these health challenges can also lead to financial setbacks. Some individuals are lucky that they have health insurance that can cater to their needs. Are you one of these smart individuals?

You may believe that you don't need health insurance. In my opinion, this is the biggest lie you can tell yourself. It is better to have one and not need it than to need it and not have it. Life can be full of surprises.

Injuries also fall into this category. Accidents, injuries during sporting activities, or injuries that happen around the home can lead to stress. Imagine having to move around in a wheelchair for the next few months. This changes your routine and creates unnecessary stress.

Another issue with health challenges is the fact that it promotes other unhealthy situations. You find people taking up drinking and smoking to get over the pain of the illness and to also deal with depression. In issues like this, self-medication is another route that people take.

These options aren't the best solutions. What you need to do is learn more about your situation. Research on various treatments, visit a doctor for professional advice, and join support groups. If you can, perform exercises and ensure you are getting enough sleep.

These don't make the pain go away magically, but they assist in coping with your injuries or illness.

Visit people and engage in activities that make you happy.

Loss of Someone Close to You

Many people are close to you in life. These are the people who have a direct impact on how your day goes. What happens when you lose these individuals?

Here, we aren't talking about cutting off communication with a person due to their toxic behaviors. I mean, how do you handle the death of a loved one? This is one event that induces stress, and we have minimal control over these events.

Despite our acceptance that death is an integral part of life, it affects everyone differently. This can be the death of parents, a spouse, a friend, or a child. It disrupts our lives and causes indescribable grief.

Some people may express their grief as sadness, some as guilt, while others may resort to anger. This is because we have no clue how we will go through life without these individuals. It is an experience that you will have to go through sooner or later.

The journey to recovery after such loss is long and stressful. The emotions that come with this experience are overwhelming. This is a point in life when you need as much support as you can get.

This is not a journey you should take alone. Learn to rely on others. Share your grief with them. This is how you make progress toward healing.

There are people that never truly recover from the loss of a loved one. This draws them into depression and results in chronic stress that is impossible to eliminate. You must find a way to recover from this specific stressor to ensure you can move on with life.

You can enlist the services of a professional counselor to assist in getting over this loss. Also, several support groups help in overcoming this hurdle. Remember, getting adequate rest and eating right will play a crucial role during the healing process.

Changing Locations

It can be fun having new neighbors move in, but this is an action that creates a lot of stress. It results in a considerable change in your daily life.

For those of you who haven't experienced moving to a new house, I will give you an insight into some of the stress involved in this process.

One of these is finding the right place to stay. There are several apartments you have to inspect before making your choice. You are checking to find a place that is clean with the right amenities and at the right price point.

Another issue is finding a new school for the kids. This not only creates stress for you but also for the kids. They have to get used to the new school and make new friends.

Searching for a house that gives you easy access to a bus station and one that is in close proximity to shops and stores is also important. You don't want to be traveling long distances to purchase your groceries or replenish the items in your store.

If you can find a way to cope with these hurdles, don't forget that getting a new place puts a strain on your finances. This is another stressful event that you must overcome.

Packing and unpacking your possessions is no joke. You must have visited some of your friends at their new place and found out most of their things are still in boxes. Most people find it challenging to overcome the mental barrier that comes with thoughts of unpacking.

If you can hire someone to assist with the unpacking or get your friends to help, this can ease the stress you experience. It is also essential you rely on your support system to overcome the emotional stress that comes with changing locations. Talk to your new neighbors and socialize in the community.

Don't be in a rush to change your routine when you move to a new location. You need time to adjust. Doing this slowly will help minimize the stress you experience.

Your Workplace

There is a chapter dedicated to our discussion on workplace stress. This is one of the most significant stressors in the lives of many individuals. It is also the reason why some people have issues in their homes.

Poor management at work, constant criticism, overtime with no pay, and extreme workloads are some of the causes of workplace stress. The impact of this form of stress is noticeable in our relationship with others and also in our health.

Effective time management and distributing your workload can have a positive impact when dealing with this form of stress. We will discuss more on this later.

Life After Retirement

Your lifestyle after retirement is challenging to prepare for. It differs from losing a job in many aspects. For one, you don't have the possibility of getting another job.

The transition into this new lifestyle can be stressful for so many new retirees. The realization suddenly hits you that in your quest to make money, you didn't discover where your true passions lie. Your career was a significant defining aspect of your life.

To get over this sudden change, you need time. This time is crucial in changing your routine and getting to understand yourself better. The process will be a lot easier if you have a decent amount of money stashed in a savings account or 401(k).

You can engage in activities around the community to take your mind off things. Volunteering allows you to put your expertise to use.

The Addition of a Child into the Family

If you thought to adjust to your new lifestyle of doing things with your partner after marriage was difficult, then you should prepare yourself for when you have a child. At this point in life, you must carefully consider the impact your decisions will have on the life of the child. This is no longer the time to be quitting jobs because you're not passionate about it.

Unless you're fortunate, the jobs that pay enough to cater to the needs of the family won't be where your passion lies. You also have to consider the changes in your routine. Now you have to think of dropping off your child at school before focusing on other tasks for the day.

There are events that are supposed to make us happy that I have included in this section. These are the events that we often overlook when trying to figure out our stressors. The main reason why they are stressors is that they cause a change in your current lifestyle.

This is something to keep in mind when identifying your various stressors. Look for things that disrupt your current lifestyle in any way. This can be either positive or negative events.

CHAPTER 3 : LEARNING TO REMAIN CALM AND BE IN CONTROL

Anger is a feeling we experience every day at random times, merely seeing someone cut in line when you have been standing for almost an hour can make you lose your calm. This is where we all differ.

Some individuals may get angry for a brief moment before regaining their calmness. For others, they might go completely out of control. This is why it is necessary to understand how angry you are in any situation.

Your anger is a potential cause of stress in your life. In this chapter, we will be taking an in-depth look at how anger and stress are related.

Despite some of the issues with anger, it also offers some benefits to you. If you're in doubt, go through the next section.

Benefits of Anger

It Gives You a Sense of Control

When you get so angry and become confident enough to tell an individual off, then you get a feeling of being powerful. Although this may not be true, your anger at that moment makes it possible for you to become forceful and assertive. It allows you to be in charge if only for that brief moment.

People Respect Anger

As a form of response, people tend to respect your decisions when you're angry. The reason is that others assume that you are standing up for yourself when making these decisions. It is you being confident and assertive in a manner that prevents others from taking advantage of you.

You Get Positive Results

I'm sure this won't be a surprise to you. When you're angry, you usually get the results you want. If you portray yourself as the nicest person with people-pleasing habits, people tend to trample on your boundaries and ignore your decisions.

This doesn't apply when you're angry. At this point, you become intimidating and willing to confront others to get what you desire.

It Gives the Assumption that You are Working on Your Stress

There is usually a situation that triggers your stress. When you get angry, it is a response that promotes the assumption that you're channeling your energy toward resolving this situation. Anger prompts you to take action and quickly solve the problem at hand, even though forcefully.

Despite these benefits that make anger appealing, there are more adverse effects of this response. Understanding these negative sides of anger will make it easy to understand why you need to control it.

Problems with Anger

It Becomes Difficult to Make Friends

Developing a strong bond with others becomes a problem when you give in to your anger with ease. This lack of friendship makes things more challenging when you need to rely on your support system to overcome stress.

You Tend to Hurt Those Around You

This is one of the ways anger makes it difficult to build an effective support system. While you may be the most fun person to be around when you're calm, your anger might be destructive. You can end up physically or mentally abusing the ones you love and promoting conflict in the home due to this anger.

It Promotes Destructive Habits

Smoking, overeating, and drinking are some of the behaviors that you may adopt due to anger. Regardless of the reason, which is often in a bid to calm down, these behaviors have a negative impact on your health.

- The effect of anger on your stress levels
- Is there a right time to express anger?

Keeping your Temper in Check

Have you ever tried punching a wooden door just for fun? You feel the pain in your knuckles when taking this action. On the other hand, it is possible to punch through the same door when you lose your temper without feeling any form of pain.

This is why you need to learn to keep your temper in check.

Engaging in Anger Management Exercises

Anger management exercises are techniques that can assist you in remaining calm when you find yourself in stressful situations. There are numerous anger management exercises that you can try when you notice yourself getting angry. Here are some of the exercises that can help:

Progressive Muscle Relaxation

When you are getting angry, or under stress, one of the clear signs is muscle tension. Once you notice this sign, it is essential that you use progressive muscle relaxation exercises to maintain your calmness.

Applying this technique is straightforward. It requires you to focus on one muscle group of the body and then relaxing it. As soon as you relax this muscle group, you move on to another. You can start the process from the muscles in your toes and work your way to the head or the other way around.

This process will help you maintain your calmness just before you lose control.

Don't be Idle

This is merely a way to tell you to engage in regular exercises. This is important if you want to get effective anger management results or reduce stress. There is no shortage of physical activities to engage in when you're trying to control your anger.

You can take a walk, joy, or go for a ride on your bicycle. This will make it possible to overcome your anger.

Identifying Your Anger Triggers

Many people don't know the things that easily irritate them, which makes it challenging when dealing with their anger. There are specific triggers that are sure to make you lose your cool. Learning these triggers is an excellent way to prevent anger from taking control of your life.

All you need to do here is take some time to reflect on past instances in which you lost control. There are certain events you recall always makes you get angry. This event is one of your triggers.

There are also certain situations that you subconsciously avoid. These are undoubtedly some situations that quickly get you angry. Some individuals avoid walking past the desk of a particular coworker because they always do something annoying when they do. Others avoid driving to work because they aren't patient enough to wait in traffic.

Stop Replaying a Past Event Continuously

Some events make you angry, which you can resolve. It is common for individuals to engage in a process known as ruminating or dwelling. This involves repeating that same situation over and over in your head.

The problem with this action is that you make it easier for your anger to linger longer than necessary. This, in turn, causes your anger level to rise more than necessary. You must stop this process and move past such incidents.

Changing your perspective is one way to move on with ease. Is there any positive side to such a situation?

Learning to Listen

The problem with anger is that it clouds sound judgment. Situations that shouldn't have lasting consequences become significant issues because you keep exhibiting the jumping conclusion bias. You keep making assumptions without any substantial evidence to prove it.

You need to stop. Once you can stop yourself, then also make it a habit to listen to others in an argument. This is the only option available if you want to resolve the situation amicably with the right responses.

You don't have to make rash decisions; you can choose to take a walk to clear your head. This will help you respond better to the conversation.

Setting Expectations to Help in Remaining Calm

Why is it so easy to get angry when standing in line to purchase on a regular day, but you remain calm when waiting in line to get Black Friday deals? The reason is simple. You already expect the situation you find yourself in during the latter.

This is an excellent tip that can help you overcome your anger. You need to set appropriate expectations. Your anger may often be due to unrealistic expectations you set for the world around you.

If you expect others to be nice to you because you're nice to others, then you'll be surprised by what is to come. In your interaction with others, you tend to judge them based on your expectations. It is easy to become frustrated and angry when others don't meet up with these expectations.

In creating realistic expectations, the first step is to understand that people see things from a different perspective. It implies that the things they prioritize will differ from yours.

There are some questions that you can ask yourself to help you determine if you have realistic expectations. These include:

- Do you think you will miss the train or bus someday?
- Do you believe that a neighbor may decide to play loud music that will interfere with your work?
- Have you considered the possibility of your laptop crashing when you need it the most?
- Do you think of a day when you will be out of your job?
- Do you expect a loved one to disappoint you at some point?

These are simple questions that can help you set realistic expectations. In truth, you may never experience some of these situations in your lifetime. At the same time, if you give a straight 'No' as your answer to more than one of these questions, then you may have unrealistic expectations.

If you fall into this category, then you are likely losing yourself to anger because of the expectations you have of the world. To prevent this, you must accept that there are things that are beyond your control. It is also essential you prepare for these situations.

Most people prepare for a time when they don't have a job to go to. This is why they set aside a specific amount to put into a savings account. No one wishes for this situation, but everyone expects it to happen sooner or later.

Working on Your Short Fuse

What exactly is a short fuse? To identify this, you must determine how quickly you react when faced with a frustrating or unpleasant situation. If it only takes a few seconds or minutes for you to lose your calm, then you have a significant problem on your hands.

So how do you work on this short fuse? There is a way to achieve this goal that I will introduce to you. This is through this method known as "paradoxical intention."

Paradoxical intention refers to a process in which you face your fears or problems head-on. In this case, this implies putting yourself in situations that promote your anger and stress. This can help in extending your fuse, developing patience, and overcoming anger.

Various situations can induce an anger response. As I mentioned earlier, standing in line for too long can be one of these situations. Another situation is dealing with a salesperson who lacks the experience to respond to you swiftly.

To achieve the goal of extending your fuse, then if you find yourself in a position to choose between two lines to join, pick the longest line. Since you regularly get frustrated and angry waiting in line, then you can work on your fuse by doing this frequently.

The same applies to dealing with an inexperienced salesperson. Make it a habit to pick the newest employee to help with your purchases. This will help you develop more understanding and patience.

Anticipate Various Anger-Provoking Situations and Rehearse Your Responses

This is something you should plan for when setting your expectations. You should expect to find yourself in a situation that will make you lose your temper. How do you get over such cases?

Preparing for such situations can have positive results. This preparation gives you a chance to evaluate a situation beforehand. Anger is a rapid response that doesn't give you enough time to perform proper evaluation and assessment.

Anticipation is crucial if you are to overcome this anger response. This is possible if you know the potential situations that can cause you to get angry. Working with these triggers in mind is your only option.

You are going to be coming up with various sentences that you'll say to prevent you from losing your temper. Examples of such situations can be an interaction with a coworker who doesn't try to work with other members of the team. This is one cause of disagreements in the workplace.

While rehearsing and choosing the right words to say, you should also expect the other person to get angry. Replay the scenario numerous times in your head and visualize how you can handle it without it escalating. This will better prepare you for real-life situations and help you get by without getting angry.

Another way to do this is to mimic a character you love. There are numerous TV shows that you can teach you a thing or two about anger management. These characters often engage in self-talk that helps them remain calm when they find themselves in such unpleasant situations.

Do you know any character that you can copy to help you remain calm? What will they say in such situations?

Find Humor in Anger Provoking Situations

When managing anger and stress, you can't undermine the importance of humor. Finding humor in situations that trigger your anger can help you minimize the effect of the situation. Laughing at past mistakes or your current situation is a way to eliminate the anger and stress that come with these situations.

Another alternative is to read books that contain humor. Make these books about the lives of others.

This makes them relatable and promotes a feeling of acceptance in you.

Talking to friends can help. Seek out those friends who have a way to find humor in everything. The chances are they will find something absurd in your situation to make you laugh about it. This can be an excellent way to lose the anger that comes with the situation.

To simplify your task, you must make humor a part of your life. That means developing a sense of humor. As you maintain it, you find out that you can easily rely on it when you find yourself in overwhelming, stressful, and anger-inducing situations.

CHAPTER 4 : DEALING WITH WORKPLACE STRESS

Workplace stress has a significant impact on many individuals today. The lack of proper management of this form of stress usually has adverse effects on the personal life of the person involved.

This form of stress is a serious issue because many employers promote it in the workplace. This is due to the kind of communication they adopt, the management style or culture, and the workload they put on the employees. Management styles differ depending on the company you work in.

Some managers engage in acts of harassment and bullying in their bid to get the results they desire out of employees. The effect of this style of management on the employees becomes noticeable when compared to other organizations where the work environment is built on consideration and care.

The type of job you have also has a significant role to play on your stress levels. Jobs that require your daily interaction with clients and other members of the public usually pose a higher risk to your stress levels. This is why you must take steps to ensure that you know what a job entails and are confident in your ability to perform these duties before accepting it.

There are various causes of workplace stress and strategies that can assist you in dealing with then. This is what I will be focusing on in this chapter.

Actions from a Boss That Can Cause Stress

Your boss plays a significant role in how the workplace can induce stress in your life. This is a person that you must interact with every day. Let us take a look at how they can be a thorn in your side:

Micromanagement

Micromanagement is a style of management that involves a manager who is continually trying to control the work of his/her subordinates. They do so by observing everything you do, paying attention to details, and exerting control by making too many changes to the work.

The changes they make have a significant influence on the project. They make it seem more like the work of the micromanager than yours. This form of management usually has adverse effects on the employees in direct contact with the micromanager.

There are several ways by which micromanagement from your boss can lead to workplace stress. These include the following:

A Drop in Your Productivity

Micromanagement involves being under the control of your boss. This means that they can choose to make changes to your projects by tweaking it to suit their tastes. Following these changes, there is usually a need for you to readjust to get a proper handle on the new details of the project.

Adapting to these changes requires you to slow down on your progress. This interferes with your workflow and makes it difficult for you to work harder on your project. This results in a drop in your productivity levels.

Another reason for this loss of productivity is that constant changes by your boss will cause you to question your skills and abilities. Once you lose confidence in your skills, you will start to rely more on the input of your boss before going ahead with your projects.

This is a form of conditioning that causes you to lose what makes you unique in the workplace. By staying on at this job, you find out that you're always struggling to meet deadlines while providing low-quality results on various projects.

You Stress Over Your Job Security

When you're being micromanaged, you already start losing the things that make you stand out in the workplace. Combine this with your low productivity in the form of missed deadlines and subpar results, and then fear will steadily creep into your work.

You start to stress over the possibility of losing your job every time you walk into the office environment. You worry about the chance of getting a demotion since you don't measure up to the standards of your current position.

It Makes it Difficult to Work with Others

Micromanagement in the workplace is not the right style if you want to foster good teamwork. There is a strained relationship between colleagues who work under a micromanager. Instead of getting opportunities to work on projects with other members of a team, they have to limit themselves to working with the micromanager.

While teamwork is essential in promoting communication and assisting in achieving goals at a much faster pace, micromanagement has the opposite effect. With the constant criticism you have to endure, it becomes impossible to delegate your tasks to other individuals who are better skilled in an area.

There is no opportunity for you to collaborate with others to solve a specific problem or come up with new ideas to move the company forward. Since micromanagement does an excellent job in making you feel underappreciated and undervalued, the effects will take a toll on your mental health.

It Decreases Your Morale

Another effect of micromanagement is the loss of independence when performing your duties. This is because you can't make decisions without consulting your boss. This is a situation that decreases your morale toward work.

As a result, you lose the drive to be creative or try harder since you will still get criticism from your boss. This criticism can be interpreted as the micromanager shredding the confidence you have in your knowledge and experience to bits. At this point, you are no longer coming to work because you want to, you're simply after the paycheck at the end of the month.

It Causes Stress in Your Home

The frustration of working with a micromanager can stick to your like a sore. This makes it easy to bring this work-related stress into your home. You become a thorn in the sides of your loved ones due to this experience.

You're constantly having a hard time coping in your workplace. To let your frustrations out, you give those around you a hard time. In the end, what you have is an irreparable relationship due to issues at work.

It Creates Distrust

Since it becomes clear that your manager or boss has no confidence in the work you do, it is a sign that they don't trust you. In the same regard, you also lose your trust in this individual. This lack of trust can make interactions between both parties more stressful than it should be.

As the micromanager gives you the impression that your initiative and knowledge doesn't get the desired results, you seek out new avenues where your expertise will be appreciated. This results in stress as you dedicate your time and energy to looking for a better opening in other companies.

Employee Turnover Will be on the Rise

Another way micromanagement can create stress in your workplace is an increase in employee turnover. This can affect you from two different perspectives. The first is the possibility of you quitting your job in search of something better.

The second is other employees in the company leaving in search of other opportunities. The stress that comes with this situation is apparent in the need to retrain new staff. Although the company may take care of the initial training, you will also play a role in helping recruits get a better understanding of their job.

When you have to repeat this process often, it makes it difficult for you and other members of the department to gain any form of momentum. You always have to slow down for others to catch up. This limits what you can achieve while working at the company.

Sooner or later, this increased turnover might have you out of a job. This is because it has the potential to cause the company to go downhill. Preparing for this potential collapse can also be a stress-inducing situation.

It Promotes Health Problems

In addition to stress, there are other health issues that you can experience due to micromanagement. These issues often result from your search for coping strategies. It might make you start overeating, smoking, or drinking to get over the problems plaguing you at work.

If you're able to prevent yourself from engaging in these non-destructive habits, you may still find yourself having challenges. You can experience problems with your sleep, an increase in blood pressure, or an increase in the chances of having a heart attack.

The chronic stress you experience can also lead you to depression and lower self-esteem. This is often the case when the constant abuse from the micromanager is emotional or verbal.

Inability to Recognize Your Effort or Provide Rewards

As an employee, it is your job to put in your best and offer the best results. This is the reason why you are hired in the first place. Despite this, it also helps to gain recognition for your hard work.

It is common to find yourself in a situation or work environment in which your employer, boss, or supervisor doesn't recognize your efforts. This can adversely affect your output.

This is an action that results in workplace stress for most employees. The negative effect of this is that it may hinder any future performance of the employee in question.

Turning Deaf Ears to Employee Opinions

Have you been turned down when trying to give an opinion at work? Depending on how this happens, it can create work-related stress. Imagine your boss throwing your opinion out the window during a staff meeting. It creates a feeling of incompetence that leads to stress.

It is usually disrespectful when your boss outrightly discards your opinion. This means they don't even take the time to see things from your perspective. A place where you feel your contributions are irrelevant won't be appealing to you.

Engaging in Acts of Discrimination

When in a work environment, you expect everyone to be equal. This is often not the case in most work environments. There are usually subtle acts of discrimination.

This is a common occurrence when you are sent to a different company as a representative. You might end up receiving treatment that makes it clear that you are an outsider. You don't get an invite to meetings, your input is rarely needed on projects, and you are always the last to receive relevant information if at all it reaches you.

These actions induce stress and can discourage you from performing your duties. Several employees quit their jobs to escape the discrimination they go through. Discrimination can occur in your current workplace in situations where you get a transfer.

If your boss isn't allowing you to blend into the new environment, it can have a negative impact on your stress levels.

Inability to Give Clear Expectations

There are bosses out there that don't give expectations to their employees. This is common among those that are supervisors or managers in a company. They simply give orders.

Through these orders, they do their best to control the actions of those working under them. One reason for this is to prevent anyone from taking their position. Since they limit any form of unique input from any employee, it helps in helping them retain the privileges that come with their current status.

In other cases, a boss who has no ulterior motives but simply lacks the ability to give clear expectations also causes stress in the workplace. There is no possibility of offering your best performance when you don't have an idea of what you ought to achieve.

When a lack of clear expectations leads to issues in the workplace, you can expect the blame to rest on the employees. This can lead to stress since there are usually consequences in one form or the other.

Lack of Interaction and Transparency with Employees

Interaction with employees gives room for a lot of progress in the workplace. A lack of this interaction promotes several negative situations. One reason why some bosses do this is to maintain their supremacy in the workplace.

They are of the opinion that interacting with employees, maintaining transparency, or being open in their decision-making processes, a time will come when an employee will reject such decisions. As a result, others will take the same route in the future.

This action not only creates stress in the workplace, but it also strains the relationship between the boss and other employees. The employees will resent any boss that operates in this manner. There is another issue that creates stress when there is no interaction.

A lack of interaction means your boss can't know the areas in which your strengths lie. That means you will be getting projects that are outside your area of expertise regularly. This will lead to difficulties in completing tasks and meeting deadlines.

Such a situation is stress-inducing since you always have to worry about not meeting deadlines, and there is a sudden lack of interest in your work. This is because you have to work on something unrelated to your skills. As a better alternative, you may choose to quit your job.

Creating a Hostile Environment Where They Rule Through Fear

The type of work environment that your boss creates has a massive impact on your stress levels. There are several employers or bosses that create a work environment in which they maintain their operations through fear. They always make sure they are dominating toward employees.

This is how they ensure that they can get an employee to do what they want, anytime they want it. This method is also an effective means of suppressing criticism and creativity in employees.

If this explains your current workplace, then it is enough reason to have work-related stress. Not only are you constantly being prevented from expressing your creativity, but you are also in constant fear of what might happen the next time you are at work. Will it be your turn to get told off in front of your colleagues next?

Another way this induces stress is a constant worry about job security. There is a possibility of getting fired if you try standing your ground. In a bid to avoid these situations, you might also consider quitting and getting another job. This is another everyday stress-inducing situation in your life.

Steps That You Can Take to Prevent Stress from Difficult People

You need to take proper measures if you want to minimize the stress you experience due to individuals that prove difficult. To give you a better handle on this situation, follow these tips:

Create Boundaries

Difficult bosses and people often have behaviors that make them the way they are. This is the reason that you find an interaction with them challenging. An effective way to deal with them is to set boundaries.

A boundary is an effective way to prevent any form of contact between you and this individual. The boundary will include various steps you take that will create a distance between both parties. This develops into a form of fence that they won't want to cross.

Learn the Triggers for Their Unwanted Behaviors

Everyone has something that makes them tick. This is the same with difficult bosses. There is always a trigger that makes their unpleasant side take center stage.

Finding out these triggers can help you avoid any issue with your boss. Minor things like a typo can make a boss lose their cool. If your boss exhibits this trait, then be sure to double-check your work or reports before turning it in. Noticing these triggers can save you from a lot of stress in the future.

Don't Let Their Actions Get to Your Work

A problematic boss doesn't always have to be a micromanager. This individual may be someone who doesn't acknowledge you or one that is always criticizing your work. Many people usually try to get even with such bosses.

To achieve this, they will resort to delaying projects, extending their breaks, or merely taking multiple days off to treat themselves. This is not a great way to handle a demanding boss.

What this does is to ensure that you keep piling up your workload. If you're unlucky, you might also receive your termination letter as an early Christmas gift.

Other Causes of Workplace Stress

Although your boss may be the main reason why you experience stress in the workplace, there are other causes of workplace stress. These may be due to an indirect impact from your bosses and colleagues. The following are some obvious reasons for workplace stress:

Your Age

Getting a job can be difficult when you go past the age of 40. This is defined as ageism. You will notice this in the way employers prefer to recruit individuals who are much younger during their hiring processes.

The main issue with ageism is that it often results in a lack of job security for the older generation. This means an increase in stress levels in such individuals.

Duration of Work Hours

The length of your work hours is an essential part of your work-life. This duration is a determining factor in how much you take home when you receive your paycheck. So how does this result in workplace stress?

There are two ways by which this can result in stress. The first is having your work hours reduced. There are lots of bosses who engage in this unfair practice. This is an action that they take to avoid paying their employees any form of benefit due to the additional hours.

The second occurs in a situation where a boss gets employees to work additional hours without pay. That means you are going overtime without any extra payment. This overtime will take its toll since it also limits your ability to effectively take on another job to make a little extra if necessary.

Since health is a priority, overtime can also result in burnout if you don't take proper care of yourself.

Inability to Separate Work from the Home

Your work life is distinct from your personal life. This is a fact that you must accept. Regardless, many individuals still have an issue separating their personal life from work life.

With advancements in technology, it is easier for an employer or supervisor to reach out to an employee despite the distance. It is possible for an employer to get an employee to work remotely while monitoring their progress from anywhere in the world.

In some cases, there is an urge to go through your work emails when you are at home after work or during the weekends. It is common to feel a sense of guilt when you fail to go through these emails. This inability to completely disconnect from work and the continuous disappearance of work life/personal life boundaries can lead to stress.

Excess Workload

An increase in workload results in a direct rise in pressure. Too much pressure from your workload and it will cause burnout. This is a significant cause of stress in the workplace.

The impact of this excess workload is more noticeable in organizations that provide minimal resources and low budgets for the employees to work with. This is a stressor that you can link to ineffective management by the supervisor.

General Tips to Avoid Workplace Stress

Request for Clear Requirements on Every Task

When you're assigned a place in the workplace, always ensure you get all the requirements from your boss. This will give you a guide on what they want to get out of the project. It can also help you avoid any issues later on.

Remove anything that distracts you in the workplace

You will keep experiencing workplace stress if you don't make sure you can maintain your focus in the workplace. To maintain focus, you must make sure to remove all your distractions. What keeps taking your attention away from work?

Do you always give in to the urge to check your social media pages? Are you constantly scrolling through the pages of a magazine you have on your desk? Is there a colleague in the next cubicle who you enjoy conversing with?

Finding a way to let go of these distractions will help you minimize the stress you go through in your workplace. You find it easier to finish projects before deadlines while providing your best work on every project.

Look for Options to Work from Home

There are times when the work environment doesn't promote effective working habits. You can try looking for opportunities to work from home. This is an option that reduces stress in several ways.

You don't have to rush to catch the bus, you aren't frustrated by the morning traffic, and you avoid dealing with difficult colleagues. Despite the potential benefits of this alternative, many bosses don't provide this option to their employees.

Do Your Research

This tip is for anyone who is trying to get a new job. Before you accept that offer, make sure you take your time to perform extensive research. You can find an opportunity to talk to the staff of the company.

Your goal is to glean as much information as they are willing to give you. Try to learn more about the boss you will be working with. Are you going to be getting into another less than ideal situation again?

Your Approach Toward Problem Solving Should be Systematic

The projects and tasks that you handle in your workplace are all problems that you must solve. The way you handle these problems affects your stress levels. Taking the systematic route in problem-solving will help ease the burden.

The first thing you should do is to identify the exact problem you intend to solve. Also, break it down into simpler parts that make it more manageable. Once this is complete, your next step is information gathering.

Without information, you will keep going in circles without making any actual progress. Information is crucial in coming up with new and practical ideas. This is due to the multiple perspectives it offers.

You notice you are making positive progress in handling your task without too many setbacks. Now, it is time to go back in time. Have you dealt with a similar task in the past? Did you come up with a unique solution for solving the problem?

With everything you have in place, you can choose the best path to take in achieving the results you desire.

Make Changes to Your Behavioral Approach

Your behavior toward work can be the reason why you experience stress. It is time to make the necessary changes. One of these is learning to say no, which I will discuss in detail later.

Another step to take is to assess your expectations in the workplace. Are you being realistic? If you're always considering the worst case, then you will be inducing stress into your life. The same applies if you think everything should go according to your plan.

A behavior that is common to many people in the workplace is noticeable in their use of free time. Most people use it for unnecessary activities. If you want to reduce your workplace stress, then get productive in your use of free time.

If you keep holding grudges in your workplace, then you're only making things worse for yourself. Everyone should act maturely in the workplace. The best way to get people to treat you right is to be direct and open when resolving conflicts. You also need to stop blaming others for every unpleasant event you go through.

Another behavioral trait that gets a lot of people in trouble in the workplace is procrastination. Do you procrastinate? If you're still doing so, then this is probably the main reason why you always stress over meeting your deadlines. Find out how you can stop this from affecting your performance.

Make Positive Lifestyle Changes

Many of the tips I give you in handling workplace stress are closely related to changes in your lifestyle. Regardless, this section focuses on the change of specific actions that are more identifiable as habits. Here is a list of these habits:

- Smoking
- Consuming Excessive Caffeine
- Not eating a balanced diet
- Not getting enough rest
- Avoiding exercises

If you can make a change in these areas, then you can turnaround your life in a manner that also reduces workplace stress. Being optimistic in your approach toward work and other things in life also gives you an upper hand in overcoming stress. Negativity is one thing you must avoid.

Still on negativity, worrying about unimportant things can cause stress in the workplace. Stop dwelling.

If you must eat out while at work, make sure you don't take foods that contain excess salt, saturated fats, sugar, chemicals and white flour. Your health is crucial if you're to work at peak performance for years to come.

CHAPTER 5 : HOW TO CONTROL STRESS IN LIFE

Stress control is your duty and no one else can help you achieve it. Knowing the right actions to take matters a lot in getting what you really need. In this chapter, you will learn the steps and also habits that can help in controlling the steps you experience.

Simple Actions You Can Take to Reduce Stress

Learning to Express Gratitude

Showing gratitude is a simple action that has several benefits. It can help in reducing the risks of loneliness, anxiety, and depression. Understanding what gratitude is all about can help combat stress in your life.

For various individuals, gratitude may mean something different. To some individuals, gratitude may be a show of thankfulness anytime they avert a dangerous situation. To others, it can be simply saying thank you to another individual for offering a service or giving a gift.

In another less appropriate manner, gratitude is identifiable in an individual that is grateful that they are better off than others. This can be in terms of success, finances, physical appearance, and so on.

In this context, our interest lies in how gratitude can help to relieve you of stress in your life. There are various ways by which this can happen. One of these is noticeable in how gratitude can help change your mindset from negativity to positivity.

Focusing on the negative parts of your life is one of the reasons why you may feel stress. Through gratitude, you focus more on the positive experiences in your life. This minimizes stress and helps you feel good about yourself.

In feeling good about yourself, gratitude can also get you to notice those around you. The ones who do the most for you and love you unconditionally. By recognizing these individuals, you can avoid thoughts that aim at putting you down or promoting negativity due to loneliness.

In adopting the tend and befriend response, showing gratitude to others will also help in improving your relationship with them. They will start feeling better about you, and this will prompt them to get closer to you.

Although it can be challenging to identify the effects of gratitude on stress, this simple action can make you more satisfied with your life and happier. These are qualities that reduce stress.

Achieving Your Goals

Goals are essential if you want to get ahead in life. This is when you can accomplish these goals. Your inability to meet these goals can have a negative effect on your life.

Your goals can be separated into simple and major goals. Going jogging in the morning is a simple goal while buying a new house is a major goal. In working toward a major goal, it is possible to split it into simple goals that you can easily accomplish.

Many people experience burnout when working toward major goals due to their inability to break it down into simpler parts. You can notice this when working toward a project in the office. Large projects often have a deadline before which they must be completed.

As the deadline draws closer, it becomes difficult to take breaks, socialize, or even go to sleep. If you try to take a break, you feel like you are throwing away precious time. On the other hand, you are unable to work effectively due to fatigue.

These can promote stress in your current situation. To ease the process, you must set small, achievable daily goals. This applies to every area of your life.

Achieving a goal will grant you a sense of fulfillment, and it makes you feel better about yourself. It is also much easier to work toward a larger goal if you can break it down. By doing so, you can avoid the burnout that occurs when putting in too much work.

Through daily goals, you have the goals that you must achieve for each day. Once you realize them, you have the rest of the day to socialize and rest. The next day, you work on a new set of goals and achieve them with ease.

The benefit of this is that you are less overwhelmed by your larger projects, and you minimize the stress you experience.

Do Something Good or Help Others in Need

Stressful situations promote negative thoughts in your life. It is also identifiable in decline in mental health and a change in mood. To overcome these stressful situations, doing little things for others can help.

These actions serve as coping strategies that can make you feel better about yourself. In addition to promoting better mental health, helping others can also improve the positive emotions you experience overall. There are different ways to help others when choosing this option as a means to overcome stressful situations.

Simple acts like sharing things with others count. Are you an excellent baker? Then you can decide to bake a cake and share it with your colleagues at work. These are little acts of kindness that go a long way.

Volunteer work is another avenue by which you can help others while simultaneously helping yourself. If you're a professional in any field, then there will surely be a need for your skills. Visit any non-profit in around your location and offer your services.

If volunteering is demanding more time than you can spare, then opt for something simpler. Donate to any charity you like. Your money will do a lot in helping those in need.

Your gestures shouldn't be left out when you decide to do something good. A simple smile can brighten up the day of another individual. Doing good isn't always about giving the most money or spending the most time with a person. Your gestures and hugs are also very impactful.

Habits That Can Help in Managing Stress

A habit is a practice that you engage in regularly. It is an integral part of your life. In dealing with stress, developing certain habits can help relieve it.

There are several actions that you can turn into habits when working toward overcoming stress in your daily life. Here is a look at some of the best habits you can develop toward achieving this goal:

Exercising Frequently

Many people consider exercise to be a stressful activity, and this is the truth. Despite this, exercising is an excellent habit you can develop when trying to overcome negative stress. You can consider exercising to be a form of eustress.

Through regular exercise, you can help the body relieve any form of mental stress it is undergoing. You must perform these exercises regularly if you want to enjoy the benefits.

In overcoming mental stress, exercising can help you develop confidence in your body. It is also necessary to promote a better quality of sleep. Stress is one of the main reasons why people have difficulties getting a good night's rest.

Another benefit of exercising is the reduction of stress hormones in the body. This occurs when you engage in exercises over the long-term. Also, there is an increase in the levels of endorphins through exercise.

Endorphins are chemicals that act as a natural form of painkillers while simultaneously improving the mood of an individual. Simple activities such as jogging, yoga, walking, or dancing can fit into your exercise routine. Find an activity that you find enjoyable and use it in overcoming stress.

Eating the Right Food

A healthy diet is one of the options available when you're working on reducing stress in your life. It is easy to miss this possibility when you have other options like yoga and exercise in the mix.

In general, your blood flow and blood pressure are two areas that stress affects negatively. Over an extended period, these adverse effects can also affect your brain health. In controlling these effects, a healthy diet can provide essential nutrients.

When you decide to perform exercises to keep the body fit, you are also maintaining your brain health since exercising is a crucial factor in the anti-cognitive decline. Its role is to ensure that the blood flow to the brain is healthy. Some nutrients also maintain blood flow in this manner.

Vitamin E, polyphenols, and omega-3s are some of these nutrients. In addition to supplying the essential nutrients to the brain, they also improve the blood flow. Spinach, almonds, and sunflower seeds are some of the sources of vitamin E, while fish like tuna and salmon provide omega-3s.

For these reasons, your diet is an area that you can't overlook when dealing with stress. Considering that your schedule may not give room to prepare a healthy meal, you can start by storing fresh foods close. By having them at home, you can simplify the process.

Fiber cereals, nuts, and fruits are some foods that you can store dried or frozen. The next step is to work on your schedule. Look for ways to introduce healthy food preparation habits into your routine.

Keep Things Organized

Sometimes, the things that make it difficult to relax and those that cause stress in your life are lying around in plain sight. Having your items disorganized can cause interference while working and leave you feeling frustrated. Engaging in organizational tactics can be beneficial in eliminating stress.

Stress that results from a disorganized home or office table is usually due to the brain interpreting it as a need for more energy than you can provide. The inability to provide the necessary amount of energy will result in stress.

To retain your position of control, you must organize your surroundings. This prevents the brain from finding opportunities to wander around or scan a room for things that can serve as distractions. When organizing, you must look beyond the physical clutter you can see.

How does the desktop of your computer look? What about your email inbox? These are other areas that need organization in your life. Although it may seem insignificant, look around, is your bedroom or closet disorganized?

If your bedroom is disorganized or full of clutter, then you can expect it to affect your sleep. We will discuss more on this latter when I introduce you to the minimalist lifestyle.

Find A Support System That Works

A support system is always an excellent solution for overcoming significant issues in your life. These individuals can assist you in overcoming emotional distress. Your support system will involve reaching out to family and friends to help in developing a form of social support.

The "tend and befriend" response is a simple way to explain this need for a support system. This is a response that takes a different approach in comparison to the fight-or-flight response. The fight-or-flight response will cause an individual to choose between getting aggressive or flee anytime they come across a stressful situation.

The tend and befriend response promotes the need to reach out and connect with others when faced with the same situation. One of the benefits of the tend and befriend response is that it promotes cooperation. This is in contrast to the fight or flight response that usually results in a form of conflict.

Through the tend and befriend response, the body releases oxytocin that acts as a natural stress reliever. You can notice a tend and befriend response in a man or woman seeking out help from their partner in forming deeper bonds with colleagues at work.

Getting the Appropriate Amount of Sleep

Sleep is a crucial part of your life. During your sleep, the body has the opportunity to restore and repair its various components. Stress can make it difficult for the body to perform these functions.

You should understand by now that stressful situations usually cause the body to go into a state of alertness. This is due to the increase in heart rate, blood pressure, and cortisol levels. On the other hand, melatonin is a hormone that is responsible for regulating the sleep-wake cycles of the body.

The high cortisol levels in your body due to stress can disrupt the proper release of this hormone. Another way stress can affect your sleep is by altering the sleep cycle of the body. It promotes an increase in the time spent in REM sleep and reduces the time spent in a deep sleep.

This increase in the time spent in REM sleep is one of the reasons why you experience fatigue and daytime sleepiness. Other effects include interference to your regular sleep cycles.

There are steps you can take to eliminate the effects of stress on your sleep. One of these steps is to ensure that you make your bedtime worry-free. This means you should go through your worries before going to bed every day. A simple action like writing down these worries can help.

Meditation is another excellent option to help improve your sleep. Include it in your routine.

Developing an Excellent Sense of Humor

In a lot of situations in life, having an excellent sense of humor can come in handy. The same is true when dealing with stress. It is a simple coping strategy that you can use in fighting against the inevitable.

Stress will always be a part of your life. It will make an appearance when challenges come knocking on your door. To ensure that these challenges don't break you down emotionally or physically, a sense of humor can help. By preventing this breakdown, you can avoid the possibility of stress taking over.

There are other benefits you enjoy when you develop a sense of humor. First, it allows you to see things from various perspectives. That means you can see the positives rather than focus on just the negatives of a situation. Another advantage is that you find it easier to form a bond with others.

Bonding is a crucial part of getting over a stressful situation. It also has a massive role in the tend and befriend response. In the long-term, this will assist you in building stronger relationships.

Developing a great sense of humor can be easy if you take the right steps. There are various ways to go about this. You can start by working on your smile.

A smile is everything when working on your sense of humor. Both a real and fake smile can have a positive effect. If you have to fake a smile, in a short time, it will turn into a genuine smile.

A genuine smile will make it easier for you to burst into laughter. The next step is 'reframing.' This is an action by which you look at your situation from a different perspective.

In reframing your situation, you can choose to see it from the perspective of a friend with a better sense of humor. This means that you also have to surround yourself with others that make you laugh. We all know that, to a large extent, laughter is contagious.

To make it easier to laugh, you should find things that can induce this laughter. Comedy videos, pictures, or comic strips can play a role in developing a sense of humor. Nevertheless, don't let your laughter be at the expense of another individual.

Identifying Things That Help You Relax

Exercising in the form of yoga is now very popular around the world when discussions on ways to relieve stress come up. Yoga has a unique goal of connecting the body to the mind. This is in a bid to make you feel more relaxed.

In addition to yoga, anything that makes you relax is an excellent option for reducing stress. Another simple action like deep breathing can have positive effects on stress reduction.

Any form of stress, such as mental stress, causes the body to resort to the fight or flight mode. This happens through the activation of the sympathetic nervous system. This becomes noticeable through the rapid breathing, constriction of blood vessels, and increase in heartbeat.

To help, performing deep breathing exercises can assist in promoting relaxation responses through the activation of the parasympathetic nervous system. These exercises help you direct focus on your breathing. Paced respiration, diaphragmatic breathing, belly breathing, and abdominal breathing are all examples of deep breathing exercises.

Other relaxing actions you can take include:

- Listening to music
- Interacting with a pet

Slow-paced music, like classical music, as well as nature sounds, can have excellent relaxation benefits.

CHAPTER 6 : MINIMALIST LIFESTYLE TIPS TO HELP CONTROL STRESS

What is Minimalism?

Minimalism is a lifestyle in which you decide to live a life of less. It involves the belief that less is more. You live with less possessions, spend less, and require less which can also reduce your burden from stress due to owning excess possessions or being in debt.

There are various aspects of minimalism that can assist you in overcoming stress. This chapter will give you an introduction to some of the minimalist lifestyle steps you can take. Information on the minimalist lifestyle is a lot, so you can read more if this piques your interest.

Decluttering

Decluttering is a process by which you get rid of things that you don't need and those that don't add any form of value to your life. These things are referred to as clutter.

With the number of random situations, you face daily, it is crucial to have some places where you remain in control if you are to prevent stress in your life. Decluttering is one of the processes that can help you manage stress. It deals with controlling the possessions and items that occupy your thoughts and take your attention. Having too many possessions in your life can be a trigger for the stress you're facing.

Although decluttering is an effective way to eliminate your excess possessions, it often takes some time to complete the process. This is because some individuals have a mountain of possessions to work through when decluttering. For others, it is due to the difficulty of letting go of particular possessions.

These possessions that are difficult to let go of are usually those with sentimental value. Drawings from when your children were younger, gifts you received from someone special, and many other items fall into this category. They are items that trigger specific memories when you look at them.

Despite these attachments, letting go of these items is crucial if you are to prevent stress in your life. You should also note that discarding these items doesn't lead to regrets. It is through this path that you can open the doors for new adventures in your life.

There are various ways that you can declutter. I will introduce some of the best ways to start this process in your life today. Read on to find out the steps you can take:

Start Unsubscribing from Email Lists

There are times when you decide to subscribe to an email list to gain access to the lead magnet that is present on the site. In such cases, you don't have any genuine interest in the emails that you receive when you sign up for the list. As a result, you will keep receiving emails that you will never open.

These emails can pile up and become a distraction when searching for important messages in your inbox. The right step to take is to unsubscribe from such email lists. This will put a stop to these distracting emails flooding your inbox.

Don't Give in to Your Impulse

These are your impulses to spend money. What this means is that if you want to prevent clutter from piling up in your home, then you must stop purchasing every random thing that interests you while shopping. We will talk more about this later on.

Get Out of Toxic Relationships

The thing about clutter is that it extends beyond physical possessions. You can also eliminate clutter in the form of your relationships with others.

Certain relationships are toxic and unhealthy for your well-being.

These are the types of relationships that always stress you. If you find yourself in a relationship with someone who continually ignores your feelings, such as a narcissist, then you will find out that it will hurt you. In decluttering your life, you must make it a priority to eliminate such relationships from your life.

This also extends to friendships in which you are the only one investing emotionally and financially. True friendship requires input from both parties for it to work.

Decluttering Your Social Media

Social media is one significant time drain in your life. This is often due to the efforts we take to develop a presence on multiple social media platforms. It is common to have accounts on Facebook, Twitter, Instagram, and many more.

Having too many accounts will distract you from focusing on real-life issues. There is also the problem of comparing your life to that of individuals on social media. We often forget that people only post what they are willing to let others see.

True friendship isn't defined by the number of social media accounts you have. Pick a few social media platforms that you will operate on and limit the time you spend on these platforms daily.

Declutter Your Room

Clutter in your room has a significant impact on your sleep and your mood during the day. It means you're waking up to clutter and going to bed, thinking of the clutter around you. These thoughts will interfere with your actions during the day and also with your sleep.

Decluttering your room involves tidying it up. Fold your clothes and store them properly. Keep your shoes in the closet and do your laundry regularly.

Declutter Your Wardrobe

While decluttering your room, you shouldn't overlook your wardrobe. When you decide to go through your wardrobe, you will come across several clothes that you no longer need or wear. It is time to let them go.

These not only create clutter, but they also take up crucial space in the wardrobe. Decluttering doesn't necessarily mean throwing these clothes in the trash. You can donate them to those that are in need.

When you decide to donate clothes, make sure they are clean and suitable for wearing. The least you can do is wash and iron them before giving them out. This is a simple action that doesn't cost anything but makes you feel better about yourself.

Declutter Your Paperwork

It is easy to pile up paper clutter in the home. Your bills, old magazines, your kids' school work, and your past work documents are some of the common forms of paper clutter in the home. It is vital you find an effective way to reduce this form of clutter.

If you have an office in the home that generates a lot of paper clutter, then you should consider purchasing a paper shredder. This will help in reducing this clutter drastically. You must also come up with an effective system that you will use in filing your paperwork.

Through this filing system, it will be easy to keep your paperwork in order and also identify those that you don't need. If you can quickly get rid of paper you don't need; you don't give room for it to turn into clutter.

Go Through Your Attic, Basement, and Storage Rooms

These three places are where most people store their old possessions. Old books, old workout equipment, old electronics, and lots more items are usually found here. When was the last time you used any of the items in your storage rooms?

You can make a decent amount of money from these items if you decide to discard them. Take them to the thrift store and see how much you can get on each item. If you haven't used them in years, the chances that you will use them in another five years is low.

Benefits of Minimalism

The benefits of minimalism are also some of the simple ways by which it can help in reducing stress. Take you time to go through these benefits to understand the way it works wonders in your life.

It Helps You Focus on What is Important

Minimalism helps you identify the things that matter the most to you. When you have too many possessions, you find out that it divides your attention. You expend more energy on the things that don't matter and pay less attention to essential things in life.

Through minimalism, you can get rid of these things that don't have any significance. By reducing your material possessions, you can also reduce the stress that comes with owning these items. Stress of owning an item is noticeable in different forms.

Particular possessions need regular maintenance if they are to remain in perfect working condition.

This maintenance can require time and energy. In reality, you may not need most of these items. They are often possessions you end up owning in your bid to compete with others.

It Creates Financial Stability

Minimalism doesn't only help in getting rid of unnecessary possessions; it also prevents you from purchasing things that you don't need. These are items that cost you money in terms of maintenance and storage. There are several benefits you enjoy financially when you take this decision.

One of these benefits is that you end up increasing your savings. That is a huge plus that the minimalist lifestyle offers. If you are still working the same job while cutting down drastically on your expenses, you still have the same amount of money coming in. The difference is that unlike in previous times, you're not spending your money carelessly.

Another benefit is that it assists you in getting out of debt. One of the problems with focusing on a lifestyle of accumulation is that you often spend money that you don't have at the moment. This is through the use of credit cards or moving into a bigger house on mortgage loan.

While there is a huge possibility that you have already accumulated these debts, living a minimalist lifestyle can help you clear them much faster. This is because you have chosen a lifestyle that doesn't depend excessively on your income.

In addition to building up savings and paying off debts, you also get the opportunity to build up an emergency fund. If you engage in proper personal finance strategies, you will understand that there is a distinction between your savings and an emergency fund.

A savings refers to money that you set aside for your future or any goal you are working toward. On the other hand, an emergency fund refers to any money that you set aside to use in case of an emergency. An emergency might be in the form of hospital bills or car repairs.

Building up your savings also helps in reducing stress since you don't have to work too many jobs to make ends meet. Now, you can depend on the salary you get from one or two jobs for your survival. When you attain financial stability, it eases the stress, worries, and anxiety that usually accompany financial insecurities.

It Promotes Self-Control

A significant highlight of the world today is the consumerist lifestyle that everyone is adopting. This lifestyle is promoted by access to a constant supply of cheap items in various sectors, including the clothing industry and fast food businesses.

One of the pillars of the minimalist lifestyle is an improvement in self-control. There are several reasons why this is important when adopting minimalism in your life. One of the habits that leads you into debt and financial insecurity is your inability to say no to impulse spending.

As a minimalist, you have to learn to overcome these urges. This is where self-control becomes crucial. It assists you in breaking most of the unhealthy habits that you have developed. After breaking off from these habits, is there still any need for self-control?

There is a need for self-control if you're to avoid falling back into stressful situations such as debt. If you observe everything around you today, there is an advert in one form or the other. On your televisions, on social media, at your local grocery store, and so on. Everything and everyone is looking for a way to get you to purchase something you think you need.

This can be in the form of visual or verbal manipulation. Visual manipulation is often in the way of social media adverts, while verbal manipulation is noticeable when a salesperson tries to convince you to pick an item in addition to the one that you need. This is how they make more profits.

If you have perfected the art of decluttering without learning self-control, then you will be no different from someone that is emptying a bucket of water into a basket. It will be challenging to see the results of your efforts.

To gain self-control, you must first clearly define the things that are essential for your survival. You can consider yourself as an essentialist minimalist when you decide to only purchase and live with the essentials.

When training yourself to develop self-control, there are some steps that you can take. One of these steps is to have a list anytime you decide to go shopping. This will be a list of the items you need, and you must stick to this list when making your purchases. Know what aisle you need to go to when searching for a specific item on the list.

Another step is to limit the amount of money you have on you. How much will the items on the list cost? Determine this amount and take that specific amount along. If there is a need to take additional money, then it must be for essential things like refueling your vehicle.

By taking these actions, you can prevent yourself from worrying about how you spent all the money that was supposed to last a month. Self-control assists you in developing healthy spending habits. By learning to say no when a salesperson tries to convince you to make a purchase, you can also learn to say no when others ask you for favors at inconvenient times.

Learning to Prioritize

One of the reasons you end up in stressful situations is because you try to do too many things at once. This is what we call multitasking. In your defense, you may adopt the argument that you're trying to be more productive when multitasking. Have you ever assessed yourself when multitasking?

When you take time to assess your performance while multitasking, it is common to find out that you're working below your peak. Contrary to popular opinion, multitasking isn't the best solution. This process causes you to overexert yourself.

It leads to more stress and reduces the quality of your output. This leads to an unhealthy state of the body both physically and mentally. A better alternative that you learn from minimalism is to prioritize.

Setting your priorities makes it easy to achieve more. It is also a vital step to take in eliminating the stress that you experience when you decide to multitask. In the worst case, multitasking will result in burnout.

By shifting to the approach in which you work on things according to your priorities, you can give your full attention to a project. This way, you are sure of getting the best results from your efforts. You can allocate more resources and time to completing these priorities. This minimizes the possibility of getting overwhelmed while working.

In setting priorities, there is usually a need to make choices. It can often involve deciding not to go on that evening outing with your friends to complete your project. This is to prevent you from delaying your work till the deadline gets close.

Remember, you must always set aside the appropriate time to socialize and relax your body. The goal is to tackle the things that can lead to stress first while working on minor things after. This way, you still get time to enjoy life after completing the various goals that you have set.

Eliminates Distractions

In addition to the physical impact of minimalism, it also affects your digital life. You might often come across discussions where people say that they are digital minimalists. This is another way to eliminate stress, especially in your work environment.

One of the primary reasons why we develop work-related stress is often due to our inability to meet deadlines. As the deadlines draw closer, the project you are working on suddenly becomes a lot more overwhelming. This is where you have to take time to assess your time management strategies.

What are the things taking your time? The most straightforward answer to this question will be distractions. So what exactly are your distractions in the workplace?

Having access to the internet isn't supposed to be a bad thing, but it can pose serious problems depending on how you use it. Having an internet connection makes your smartphones and computer more entertaining than they should be, especially when you're getting bored working on a project.

Through these devices, you can quickly check your emails and go through your timelines on various social media platforms. If your original intention was to do this for just five minutes, it could easily extend to an hour. This is how you waste most of the time that you should have spent making progress on your project.

A simple approach you can take is to create time for these actions in your schedule. You can create 20 minutes time-blocks in the morning and afternoon during which you can assess your social media profiles and emails to respond to messages. When you include it in your schedule, it becomes easier to stick to the time duration compared to when you take action randomly.

CHAPTER 7 : HOW TO SUCCESSFULLY DEAL WITH CHANGES AND CHALLENGES IN LIFE AND AT WORK

The life you live is going to be riddled with changes and challenges. This is an inescapable fact. It doesn't matter if you meet someone that always seems to be happy; they are sure to have some terrible stories to tell.

The events that bring about the challenge or change usually appear suddenly. Sometimes, this makes it impossible to prepare for it. There are other times when you know it is coming, which allows you to make preparations.

The addition of a baby to the family is a change you can prepare for to an extent. You can't say the same about falling down the stairs and spraining an ankle. These are two unique ways that a change can occur.

Developing proper coping strategies is your best bet when dealing with changes and challenges. The ability to cope usually varies from one person to the other. This is why you often notice a situation where specific individuals receive praise for their resilience.

Resilience is a trait that determines how well you can cope with changes, challenges, and stress. For most people, they work on this trait to attain a level at which they aren't easily affected by the change. In most cases, this is by adopting the right strategies.

If you're one of those that keeps looking for a way to avoid change, then it is vital that you change your approach. Since it will inevitably catch up to you, it is crucial you learn ways of coping. Strategies you can adopt are what I will be discussing in the various sections of this chapter.

Practice Gratitude

There are plenty of things that you can be grateful for in life. Recalling all these things will help you better deal with changes. When you practice gratitude, you are going to remember moments when it seemed you won't be able to move forward, but you did.

These memories can give you the motivation you need to march on when you face new challenges and changes. If it is your first time taking this step, here are a few things that you can be grateful for:

- Your friends
- Your health

- Your partner
- The fact that you have a home
- The love you receive from others
- The lessons from past mistakes
- Enough money to take care of your needs
- For your job
- For safety and security, you enjoy

Put simply, anything that makes you smile is worth being grateful for. Put these things in mind when dealing with new challenges and changes in life.

Pay Attention to the Things You Can Control

In life, there is a limit to the things you can control. When a situation becomes a challenge or results in a stress-inducing change, then it is usually because it is beyond your control. We focus too much on these events, which makes it difficult for us to overcome it.

In your life, you must learn to move on from challenges and changes that you have no control over. You must fixate on the things you can control. These are the areas where your decisions are the determinants of the outcomes.

The death of a loved is a significant stress-inducing situation that is beyond your control. It is common to dwell on such events, and I'm not saying it is going to be easy to move forward. Regardless, you have no power to prevent death pr bring someone back to life.

The sooner you accept these facts of life, the faster you can get your life back on track. This is how it is with so many things we go through. At work, we complain about the personality and attitudes of our coworkers.

We often make it our mission to cause them to change. This is you dwelling on achieving something that is usually impossible. Unless the feeling comes from within, you will be pushing an immovable block in your attempts toward bringing about change.

What you can do is assess the situation and determine the things you can control. These are opportunities that promote growth in life.

Seek Out the Positives

The changes and challenges you experience don't have to be negative. There is always a positive side. You need to seek out these positives.

Your challenges can make you smarter in the way you handle money. It can also help you get closer to your family and push you into making new friends. There is the possibility of becoming more assertive and developing better habits when you go through challenges or changes.

Although we don't like changes, they often provide the opportunities we need to evolve and grow into better people. Through acceptance, you will be able to see how much improvements come with the changes and challenges you experience.

In seeking out the positives, it is essential that you also protect yourself from negative self-talk and thoughts. This is common when the challenge or change brings about a setback in your life.

What you must do to avoid negative self-talk is to ensure you don't label a setback as a form of failure. This will hinder you from adopting a positive thinking pattern.

In the end, one reason why you must embrace the idea of seeking out positives is that life is not a bed of roses. There are sure to be times when it seems like nothing is going your way. Everything you do might end up going downhill.

This will induce negativity, regardless of how optimistic you're in life. The only solution is to determine the right steps to take in dealing with this negativity. Accepting that your tomorrow will be better than today is one way to minimize the effects of negativity.

Set Your Priorities

Changes and challenges are inevitable, but they don't stop you from achieving your goals in life.

This depends on how you approach these goals. To ensure you are working toward your goals, creating priorities is crucial.

What are you prioritizing in life? You might think of making financial independence your priority, but this doesn't help when dealing with the stress that comes with changes and challenges. In my opinion, you must make your health a priority.

In the first chapter, I gave a quick look at some of the health challenges that come with stress. If you don't take steps to protect your health, then you might struggle with one of these issues.

How do you prioritize your health in this situation? One of these methods is by socializing. As social creatures, this is one step that you must not ignore. Life will be less stressful if you have someone to rely on when you're down.

There is also a need to engage in self-care. This is an action that is crucial in dealing with both positive and negative changes. This is how you promote a boost in your self-esteem and confidence. These are two factors that can help you to better deal with changes.

Don't Dwell on Social Media

When people experience changes or challenges in their lives, it is common to find them on social media in search of comfort or advice. This is the solution people adopt when the challenges involve the loss of a job or loss of a loved one. They might also try comparing their lives to that of others on social media.

In dealing with challenges and changes, you must take care when using social media. While it may seem like a good idea to create a post on social media, you need to remember that you can't retract anything you post. Even if you delete the post later, there is a high chance that someone has taken a screenshot.

You also need to be careful when comparing your life to that of your friends on social media. What they post doesn't paint the real picture of what is going on in their lives. These posts are only to make themselves look good to the world.

No one will upload a post detailing the struggles they go through in the background. If you want to deal with your challenges and eliminate stress, then social media isn't the right place to do so.

Join a Support Group

Your life is like a race. In completing this race, you need the help of others at one point or the other. Moments, when you need the help of others, include when you are facing changes and challenges.

Relying on your support group at such times isn't a sign of weakness. It is merely an acknowledgment of the fact that you understand how far you can go on your own. Your support group consists of friends, family, and other people who you trust.

These are people who will be happy to stand by your side during your trying times. They can assist in taking care of your kids to reduce the burden on your shoulders. You can also rely on your neighbors for help.

When your challenges become overwhelming, it is possible to have suicidal thoughts. Being around your family and friends can help you overcome these thoughts.

Don't be in Denial

Most of the stress that comes with changes are often a result of you trying to avoid facing these changes. By engaging in denial, you find an excellent weapon in putting off these changes. This makes things more complicated than they should be.

You only suffer more when you try to deny something that is already happening in your life. It is easy to wish for things to occur differently. Regardless, you should understand by now that the changes in life are things that you will never be able to control.

CHAPTER 8 : LEARNING TO MANAGE YOUR WORRIES AND ANXIETY

Worrying is something that we all engage in at one time or another. We worry about how we are going to feed our family, which prompts us to seek out better job opportunities. The same applies when you worry about an upcoming exam. It enables you to study much harder for the exam.

The problem with worrying is identifiable when we begin to do so in excess. Despite this increase in worrying, there is little or no action on your part to solve the problem leading to your worries. Your worrying becomes chronic, and this makes it difficult for you to find happiness or joy in other things in life.

Excess worry can result in stress and promote other disorders or conditions that are stress-related. For this reason, it is vital you control your worries to minimize stress in your life.

Defining the Good Aspects of Worry

Like stress, your worries can also be a good thing for you. This is if you can classify your worries into two categories. These are the productive and unproductive forms of worry.

The productive form of worry refers to when you engage in this act, and it promotes stress reduction while causing you to manage your life better. On the other hand, it becomes unproductive when it results in sadness, fear, and anxiety.

Productive Worrying

This is a useful form of worrying that doesn't cause you to be overwhelmed by emotions. It also eliminates the need for certainty, which is one of the stress-inducing aspects of unproductive worrying. When you worry, productively, you come up with new solutions on how to solve your problem.

Productive worrying is short-term, which doesn't make it excessive and stressful. If you come across things that are impossible to solve in your present state, you can quickly get them off your mind.

Unproductive Worrying

This is where the problem lies. The focus of this form of worrying is in seeking out outcomes with a low probability. Rather than focus on the present, you worry about solutions to problems that you out to solve later.

There is a need to control every happening in life and a refusal to accept changes and challenges as part of life. The drive to obtain perfection in problem-solving is often a reason for the stress it induces.

Why do You End up Worrying Unproductively?

There are several reasons for this. One of these reasons is depending on others for your validation. This means that you require approval from other individuals to enhance your self-esteem. Your worries revolve around the possibility of losing this approval or not getting it at all.

There is also the need to steer clear from anything that makes you uncomfortable. Your low tolerance for discomfort always comes with a price. Unproductive worrying can also be your constant focus on how bad things can get.

Worrying about failing is another common reason. We all do this in situations where others outclass our performance and abilities.

Identifying How Much You Worry

The first step you need to take is to determine the extent to which you worry. There are specific questions that you can answer, which can give you the clarity you desire. Read on to find out these questions:

- Do those that I closely relate with mention that I worry excessively?

- When considering a problem, do I focus on the worst possible outcomes?

- While worrying, do I come up with solutions or just get upset?

- Does worrying interfere with my sleep?

- Is my worrying usually over things that never happen?

- Does worrying create stress in my life?

- When dealing with uncertainty, do I find it hard to cope?

These are some questions that can help in getting a better grasp of your current situation. If most of the questions on this list have a close connection to your habits, then the stress you're experiencing is undoubtedly an outcome of excessive worrying.

Now that you accept that this is a source of your problem, you must take steps to solve it. In this section, I will introduce various steps that will help you in successfully controlling your worries.

Taking Control of Your Thoughts

Your thoughts are the roots of your worry. In getting over your worries, you must take control of your thoughts. How do your thoughts develop into worries?

When you start thinking of things such as your current situation or an event as posing more threat or danger that it does, it leads to worrying. These thoughts are usually unconscious, and they can promote stress both emotionally and mentally, depending on the response you give these thoughts.

These responses are in the form of self-talk. Give yourself positive self-talk, and you can improve your chances of overcoming the situation. When you make it negative self-talk, then you are merely going to be raising your stress levels.

To take control of these thoughts, adopting thought processes that don't promote worrying is essential. One of the ways to do this is to develop a habit of acceptance. This prepares you for the negative situations that you will surely come across in life.

Acceptance means that you don't fight your situations. Your attempts to fight your current situation is what leads you to worry about things you can't change. As you learn acceptance, you start looking for better alternatives and coping strategies to help you overcome most problems.

Finding Ways to Get Out of Your Worries

Look for Distractions

Distractions can be annoying when you are trying to work on something important. They can appear in the form of TV shows, emails, or your mobile phone. On the other hand, they can be instrumental when you want to avoid worrying excessively.

Finding something to distract you when you find yourself worrying excessively can have huge benefits. This is more effective when the distraction is something that requires your undivided attention. Many people choose to watch their favorite TV shows or funny movies to take their minds off their worries.

In my case, I opt for video games to get my mind off my worries. If you play a lot of video games, then you can imagine how much focus you need to take down a boss with three health bars. There are lots of other actions that serve as distractions, including:

- Gardening
- Window shopping
- Reading an interesting book
- Engaging in DIY projects
- Starting a conversation with others

These are some excellent tips to help you get distracted. Pick one or two that you can use to overcome your worries anytime it becomes excessive.

Talk to Someone About it

Having someone to talk to can help reduce your worries. This can be someone from your support group, including your friends and family. This person should be a good listener and also very understanding.

Sometimes, all you need to do is to let everything out. In most cases, you can see things differently as you begin to talk about it to another person.

Take a Walk

There are several health benefits of taking a walk. Choosing this option means that you will be doing yourself a lot of good in multiple areas. For one, walking is an excellent distraction to get your mind off your worries.

You can meet people on your way to converse with or find a nice store to go window shopping. As a form of exercising, walking also does an excellent job of promoting blood flow to the brain.

If your worry is work-related, then you will be happy to know that walking can also help with creativity. You will often hear a lot of writers talk about taking a walk any time they face what we call a writer's block.

In your bid to overcome stress, walking can assist you. It promotes the release of endorphins in the brain, which lowers the sensitivity of the body to stress (Rodriguez-Cayro, 2018).

Engage in Coping Self-Talk

What makes it convenient to rely on others when dealing with problems? It is because we understand that they can give excellent support. This is noticeable in their emotions, actions, and the advice they give. It is also for the same reason others rely on you when going through challenges.

When using coping self-talk, you're simply doing what you expect to get from someone else on your own. You're giving yourself the advice and support you need to get through a situation. This is one way to overcome your worries.

Coping self-talk involves coming up with excellent solutions that can help you solve the problem creating worries in your life. This is the same reason why people depend on you. They value the opinions you offer because they are helpful.

Why then, shouldn't you value your opinions? By switching your mindset to that of a problem solver, you become adaptive and accepting of your situation. This has a positive mental effect when dealing with worries.

If you want to get better results, write out the worries and the solutions you come up with. By writing them down, you give them a physical form that you can hold on to. This gives you a better sense of control that dealing with them as random thoughts in your head.

In writing down your worries, you don't need to spend a lot of time. Having a period that is as short as 20 minutes is enough to write down everything bothering you.

Here is a list of some simple coping self-talk that you can say to yourself to help you on your journey:

- There is no need to escalate this situation
- Don't jump to the conclusion that the worst will occur
- Am I getting any help from my worrying?
- What significance does this worry have in my life?
- Is there a better perspective for me to take in viewing this issue?
- Do I know any optimist? What approach will they take in this situation?
- Do I have the right emotional reaction to match these worries?
- I can cope!
- Is there any way to change this situation? Am I better off accepting?

These are some things that you can tell yourself or ask yourself to provide positive reinforcements in your life.

Avoid Taking Actions That Reinforce These Worries

Actions that promote negative thoughts are enough to feed your worries and make them get out of hand. If you're willing to overcome your worries, then you must avoid such actions. Being fearful is another action that reinforces the power of your worries.

Constant thinking about an event of the past can have a negative effect on future events. I was once in a car that lost its brakes on a downward sloping road. The slope played a role as the vehicle kept accelerating.

Thanks to the minimal traffic on the road and quick thinking of the driver who drifted the car to a halt when we got to level road, everyone escaped unhurt. Following this experience, I was having doubts about going to get my driver's license. Anytime it came up in a discussion, I had unnecessary worries about the possibility of losing control while driving.

Many people struggle with similar situations. We worry about things that may never happen again due to our past experiences. This is how we feed our worries.

You must assess your life and your worries. Are they feelings that stem from past experiences?

Stop Engaging In "What-If" Thoughts

The "what-if" thoughts are those that cause you to think of the worst outcome in every situation. It is a form of negative thinking that promotes worrying. Like in the example I gave about losing control of my vehicle, what-if thoughts played a role in my worries.

- What if I lose control of my car and get in an accident?
- What if I lose sight in my right eye?
- What if my fiancée calls off the wedding?
- What if my boss belittles me in front of the customers?
- What if there is a heavy rain right after I paint the house?
- What if I am in a plane crash?
- What if there is a fire in the home?

There are so many of these what-if thoughts that we entertain in our life. The truth is that most of these may never occur. Regardless, we still let them weigh us down.

This is you focusing on the chances of these things happening. So, what is a better way to go about these thoughts? Why not consider the possibility of these things NOT happening?

By changing how you consider a situation, you can see the positive sides of these negative thoughts. Have you considered the odds of NOT dying in a plane crash? The odds of not dying is much higher than the odds of being in a crash.

Learning How to Live with Things That Are Beyond Your Control

Excessive worrying can be attributed to situations that you can't control. As humans, we prefer to get into situations that we have little control over. This is why things beyond our control often result in stress.

Understanding that life is riddled with uncertainty is the first step in accepting things beyond your control. The comfort that comes with it also enables you to identify how much control you have over certain situations.

When you find yourself being dragged into a stressful situation, the first question you should ask yourself is how much control you have over such a situation. When you determine the level of control you have, you can reduce the extent of your worries. This has a direct effect on reducing stress.

You can use a grading system in determining the level of control you have over stressful situations. Assume you choose to grade these situations from 1 – 5, with one as situations with no control and five for those you have full control over.

A situation that is a result of the personality of another individual will have a one rating since it is beyond your control. For me, I will rate traffic as a three on my list of worries. Why? To an extent, you can alter your routes to avoid traffic.

If you do your best to exert control and there is no significant result, then you can accept the situation you find yourself in. This is often the case when I alter my route to beat traffic and find myself stuck in another on my new path.

Learn to Solve Problems

For many people, the reason why they end up worrying excessively is that they lack the motivation to solve problems. Taking the stance of a problem solver eliminates negative thinking, emotional reactions and the need for perfection, which are some of the causes of worrying.

A problem-solver is more accepting of his/her current situation. They are also more reasonable and objective in their approach toward life. Mindfulness can also assist in developing the right problem-solving approach.

Create a Time and Place to Figure Out These Worries

The same way you have a dedicated room to serve as your office in the home, there is also a need for a place to handle your worries. This is a location that you will associate with worrying. Once you get into this room, the brain knows what it means.

There are some important things you must remember when choosing a location to worry. The first is that making this room uncomfortable helps. Let it be a room that you hate being inside as this can help in preventing excessive worrying.

Your bedroom or bed isn't an option for this room. To get ahead, you can use a place that you don't visit frequently. It doesn't matter if it is a storage room; what you need is a small corner.

In this corner, you can have a chair to sit on when worrying or to come up with solutions. If this doesn't work for you, then you can choose other options. You can decide to worry on your way to work or under the shower.

Face Every Situation with Courage

Developing courage is one way to conquer your worries. It gets you to focus on the things you can control while forgetting about those beyond your influence. Another way to develop courage is to think about the worst that could happen to you.

This is a useful tip if you've been at the lowest point in life. Have you lost all your credit, possessions, and cars previously? If you have lost everything in life once and have had to start over, then that is the worst. Looking at things from this perspective will get you to understand that the outcome from facing your fears can't be worse than that experience. Besides, recalling the past means you have taken steps to ensure nothing like that occurs in the future.

Another way to face a situation with courage is to consider the alternative option. What happens if you decide not to face it? What is the cost of letting your fear overpower you?

There are many people who can't make progress in achieving their goals because they don't want to face their fears. Are you always afraid to take the next positive step? Are you missing out on opportunities in life due to fear?

CHAPTER 9 : DRAWING THE LINE TO SEPARATE YOUR HOME FROM WORK

One of the biggest struggles we have when dealing with stress is striking the perfect balance between our work life and personal life. This is a balance that is crucial if you're to avoid taking your work stress home. This is more difficult now that we have smartphones to keep us up to date on the happenings around us.

With productivity tools such as Slack and Basecamp, it seems like we are slowly losing the boundaries that separate the home from the office. This is making it possible for work to find its way into your home quickly. Without proper control measures, you will end up struggling with work stress in your home.

As this stress starts creeping in, you start becoming distracted, irritable, and negative in the presence of those that look up to you for positive encouragement. I mean your kids and partner. You're suddenly turning into an individual whose entire life revolves around work.

There are different approaches that people take when handling their work and personal life. The approach determines the possibility of creating an excellent work/life balance. These are the different routes that people take on this journey:

1. Taking their work home and completing it: This option will create a situation in which you are unable to get the required amount of rest and interferes with family interaction. Due to the lack of rest, you end up being less productive at work the next day.

2. Going home physically while your mind remains at work: In this approach, you take the critical step to go home, but you don't engage in the right strategies to mentally disconnect from work. As a result, you constantly think about the work you left behind. The issue with this approach is that you still end up being unable to get adequate rest, and it puts a strain on your family relationships.

3. Engage in the proper end of work strategies while going home to relax: This is an approach in which you avoid taking any of your work home and also take steps to ensure that you don't try to remember anything regarding work. This allows you to rest and bond with your family.

Creating a work/life balance is only possible when you can go home without having to worry about your deadlines or meetings that you have at work. It requires you to develop new end-of-work habits that will get rid of work-related stress in your life. The next section will introduce some steps you can take to ensure that this work-related stress doesn't come into your home.

Tips to Ensure Work Stress Doesn't Become Home Stress

Have Rules to Control the Use of Phones and Access to Emails at Home

One of the easiest ways by which work can creep into your home is through your mobile devices. The phone call from your boss or email from your supervisor that you don't want to ignore. These are constant reminders of your work, and they can induce stress.

We all go through these situations. You get home, have your dinner, and finally get an opportunity to relax on a couch or your bed. Then you have a random thought to go through your phone quickly.

You go through your social media accounts and then decide to also go through your emails. It doesn't matter if you're glancing through your inbox; an email from work will always get your attention. This is how you invite work-stress into your home.

Once this happens, you lose the drive to interact with your family and suddenly get into your work mode. This is where your lack of boundaries becomes glaring. In such cases, you need to put down solid rules that you must follow.

One such rule is to avoid going through your emails in the evenings or during weekends. These are periods that you must use to relax and connect with your family. Besides, a boss sending you an email after work hours shouldn't be expecting you to send a reply at that time.

Another step to take is to have a separate phone that you use for work-related communication. This is a simple rule that will yield a lot of positive results. As soon as you get home from work, you will turn off this device.

This way, you can avoid getting any form of call or notification from work. If it is necessary to leave the device turned on, then ensure it isn't somewhere that it is easy to reach. This can make it a form of distraction that you want to indulge in.

Go on a "Mental Commute"

There is also another step known as the "mental commute," which you can adopt. This is a process by which you give yourself time to disconnect from the workplace mentally. Mentally go over everything about work that is stressing you and let go of them.

This is a process that is conscious and intentional. The reason why you need this process is to ensure that while you get home physically, you also do so mentally. This implies that while you're at home, you are continually thinking of the work you left behind.

Create a Location and Time for Work Activities

The world is ever-changing, and so are the needs of the workplace. Advancements in technology make it easy for anyone to work from anywhere. Employers and clients take advantage of this by slowly creating work for others 24/7.

When you fail to draw the line and let this work creep into your home, you can also expect work stress to come with it. Are you always at the service of your employer? Do they consistently reach out to you when you're supposed to be at home?

If you keep responding to these communications from your employers in your free time, then they will assume you don't have a life. Decide on a particular time and place that you will limit yourself when working from home.

In my case, I have an office in my home that I use in instances when I must come home with my work.

I also make it a rule to set a specific time during which I work. Once this time is up, it doesn't matter what I have left to handle. I leave it for the next day.

The problem if you don't set this time limit is that you will be tempted to work for too long. It also becomes more difficult to fall asleep.

In using the home office, ensure that your work notebooks, computer, and folders are all kept here. Don't fall for the temptation to take it along to your room or the couch. Limiting yourself to a workspace has huge benefits mentally.

It gives you the motivation to work better rather than stressing over what you should have done. Leaving this room also makes it easy to accept that you're done with work for the day.

You might be wondering why I give the option of working at home despite the goal of not taking work stress home. The reason is that sometimes, your position in your office doesn't make it possible to be free completely. This is the case if you're in a management position or running your own business.

Develop a Habit That You Perform at the End of Work Each Day

There are situations when having a cue can make it easy for you to transition from the work mindset to that of your personal life. It is common to notice that the personality of most people differs when they are at work in comparison to that when they are at home.

To get them to make this shift, they develop a habit that makes the transition possible. You might have a colleague who goes straight to the gym after work. This might be a habit that they develop to get themselves to switch their gears.

In your case, you might have a specific route you always take on your way home to promote this change. For others, it can be a period of meditation. What is important is that you come up with something that works for you.

Take Advantage of the Commute Back Home

The time you spend on the way back home is an excellent period that you must utilize in dealing with work-related stress. It doesn't matter how short the time is. You can use it effectively in switching your mindset.

It is an alone time when everything can be about you. No kids are running around, colleague ranting, or boss criticizing you. Take the opportunity to unwind and start slipping into the relaxation mood. You can do this by listening to your favorite music on your phone, watching the roads as you go by, or calling a friend who you know always has something funny to say.

Anything that can make you happy is welcome. Engaging in the act of gratitude can be an excellent way to take your mind off work at this period. One thing you must try not to do is catch up on the news.

Reading the news can quickly remind you of work. Information that you find on the news often relates to different industries.

Ensure You're Getting Enough Rest

To perform your tasks for the day effectively, you need adequate rest. The reason why you should try as much as possible to avoid taking your work home is to give you enough time to rest. Through your sleep, the body has time to make repairs that are essential to your physical and mental health.

To promote a good night's rest, it is necessary to avoid exposure to blue light before bed. These include the use of your smartphones, working on your computer, or watching TV at least 30 minutes before you go to bed.

I have developed the habit of reading a book before bed. Not only does this solve my blue light problem, but it also assists me in falling asleep much faster. Create a routine out of this process to improve your sleep quality.

Use Your Vacation for Unwinding

There are periods when you can take a vacation to get away from the stress of work. Are you really getting away from work? If you are letting your employer know that they can still reach you during your vacation, then you may not get the opportunity to relax.

This is a time when you disconnect. Give yourself time and space to engage in self-care routines. The benefit of this is that it eliminates the effects of the workplace stress you're experiencing.

As soon as you resume from your vacation, you notice that you're able to work more effectively and think more creatively than before.

Take Care with What You Eat

Why are you usually very grumpy when you get home? Is there something making you unusually tired when you get back from work? One of the reasons why we often feel this way is due to what we eat or don't eat.

A lot of people work throughout the day without actually having anything to eat. Maybe only munching down on a chocolate bar or drinking a cup of coffee in the morning. This is not a good habit for you.

Hunger can make you irritable in your interaction with your family. A good idea is to pack your lunch on your way home. You can also try getting something to eat before heading back to avoid pouring your frustrations out on your partner.

Maintaining a healthy diet will ensure that you have the energy to keep working effectively. Poor performance in your work will often lead to stress.

Don't be in a Rush to Get Home

I'm not telling you to spend more time at the office. What I'm saying is that you need to enjoy the journey home. When you're in a rush to get back, everything becomes frustrating.

A minor traffic jam will create stress. The same stress will also creep in if you miss a bus. This is not a good sign when you're working toward preventing work-related stress from getting into the home.

Let Your Pent-Up Anger Out on the Way Home

It is okay to feel angry and frustrated. The only time it becomes wrong is when you lash out at your family due to your anger and frustration. The time it takes for you to get back home is the right time to let it all out.

If you're driving home, you can choose to park your vehicle to allow you to rant, vent, shout, or do anything that gets it all out. Just don't go breaking your windows or windscreen. Those are expensive to replace.

You can also choose to take a long route while walking home. In this instance, you have to vent silently. You don't want to scare other people walking on the road. As much as possible, make sure there is no need to rant or vent when you get home.

Don't Give in to Distractions at Home

When you finally get home, you're going to have your partner waiting to welcome you. If you have kids, I'm sure they will also be looking for an opportunity to interact. It is crucial you give them your full attention.

If you're absentminded in discussions with your partner, it isn't just an insult. It is also going to cause tension in your relationship. Engage in house chores to help get your mind off work matters.

Go Home Early When You're Having a Bad Day

If you're having a bad day, it will only get worse the longer you stay. These are the periods when you need the right support to get you through. You also need to rest longer to get over what is eating you up on such days.

Staying too long will worsen your mood and make you less friendly when you get home.

Don't Use Work as an Excuse to Get Out of Family Plans

Family plans include a dinner date, a promise to help your kids with their homework, or a family trip. These are events that other people involved are looking forward to. Canceling at the last minute due to work-related reasons is one way to bring work stress home.

Don't be that person who is unable to keep his/her word. Breaking a promise is also a bad habit you don't want to teach your kids or anyone around you. One of the best things about these family plans is that they often end up being much more fun that you anticipated.

Create a List of Activities That Interest You to Engage in After Work Hours

There are several activities that you can perform after work. Those that you have an interest in are usually the best. These are excellent in getting your mind off anything work-related.

The good thing about these activities is that you can do them with friends. This gives you the opportunity to socialize while blowing off steam. Include these activities in your daily routine to ensure you don't miss out on the benefits. An hour after work is enough to get the most out of these activities.

When you use these tips I have introduced in this chapter, you become a happier person. It also gives your family joy to have you around the house after your day at work. Although no one can stop you from coming home, it can be hurtful if there is no one willing to be around you.

In achieving your goal of separating work stress from your home, the person at the wheels is you. The decisions you make determine the possibility of achieving this goal.

When you decide to engage in the processes above, you have to be consistent to make them become a part of you. Turning to distractions like TV to overcome your stress won't offer many benefits.

CHAPTER 10 : TIPS TO ENABLE YOU LIVE A HAPPIER LIFE

When you finally reach a point in life when stress is no longer an issue, what do you experience? This is the moment when you experience true happiness. This is one goal that you must work toward in life.

Happiness gives you the opportunity to feel like you are alive. You don't have to worry about the minor things happening around you continually. Happiness allows you to enjoy the company of your loved ones and family.

If you want to attain this happiness, then there are some things you need to do. These are to prevent you from falling back to those things that create stress in your life. Here are some simple tips for a happier life:

Don't Take on Other People's Problems

Everyone has one problem or the other they are struggling with in life. While it is often a good idea to help others, you may be causing yourself more stress and anxiety if you're going around trying to solve everyone's problem. It is usually best to avoid getting roped into other people's issues.

You must understand that while you can offer support, you're not supposed to be the fixer. Trying to be the fixer means you see yourself as being responsible for the happiness of everyone you meet. Each person is responsible for their happiness.

When you feel this urge to fix another person's problem, remember that just like you, they have something they believe in. This is what guides them in life. Some people believe in religion, while others believe in intuition. There are many more systems that people believe in that makes them different from you.

Another thing you need to remember is the fact that it is part of life to hit the lowest points. These points are often responsible for bringing about a significant change. Trying to fix problems means that you may be a hindrance to this change that they are supposed to experience.

The last thing to keep in mind is that not everyone wants their problems to be fixed. There are many people who avoid fixing their problems to prevent change. Not everyone is ready for a change, and you can't force it to happen.

Instead of trying to take on the problems of others, practice acceptance. This practice is helpful since it also enables you to avoid worries and live a happier life. You no longer focus on the negative sides of a person; you shift your focus to the positives.

Learning When to Say No to Requests

In this book, most of the discussions revolve around stressors that are beyond your control. This may give you the impression that there are no stressors that you can control. The truth is, there are some stress-inducing situations that you can prevent.

Having control over these small parts of your life is crucial in minimizing the stress levels you have to endure. To gain this control, the vital step you need to take is to learn when to say no. With this statement, I also mean you should increase the number of times you say no to people.

One of the main reasons why some individuals have unhealthy stress levels is due to their inability to say no to others. People tend to take advantage of these individuals. The result of these actions tells on mental and physical health. Are you one of these individuals?

When you find it hard to say no to others, you start taking on more tasks than you can take care of. It is overwhelming when you need to jump from one responsibility to the other to keep up. This can induce stress and make you unhappy with your life.

The action you need to take is to decide what unnecessary workload you're picking up. Once you identify them, say no to such workloads to control your stress levels.

Our need to say yes to every request or opportunity we come across is often a silent killer. The fear-of-missing-out motivates it. You don't want to miss out on the experience, money, interaction, or fun.

While this may seem like the right choice, it doesn't let you see the value in time management. It causes you to push other things that are more important aside in favor of things that don't matter much.

When working on an important project, you might get a request for a meet-up from your friends. In order not to seem like a joy-kill, you accept the request. Through this action, you waste valuable time that you should have put to better use completing the project.

Depending on the time frame for the project, you end up struggling to meet up with the deadline. This is what happens when you don't give a thought to the consequences of your actions. The same applies to the jobs we take and the relationships we go into.

In learning to say no, you must learn to identify things that create noise in your life. The things that you can tag as noise are those that are not essential to you. These include the things that don't offer any tangible benefit.

If you want to accomplish the goal of living a happier, stress-free life, then you mustn't ignore the importance of saying no. There are numerous ways saying yes to everything can lead to stress.

Imagine getting a request from a friend to assist in a project. At that instant, you accept the request, but for the days leading up to when you have to complete the request, you feel regret. During these days, you are worried about the effect backing out of the request will have on your relationship.

These are just random thoughts that create stress. On the other hand, have you considered what happens when you say no? The answer is simple: nothing happens.

When you say no, the person requesting your help will meet another person with the same request. There are lots of other people with enough free time who will be willing to help. That is the type of world we live in.

Another way you can learn to say no with ease is if you have a clear purpose for your life. This purpose is where you're heading. Anything that doesn't help in achieving this purpose becomes noise to you.

This way, you're sure you don't miss out on anything when you say no. When you develop the ability to say no, you also lose the fear of disappointing others that usually drives you into tight corners. By eliminating this excess noise, you have a sense of clarity concerning what you want to achieve in life.

Knowing When to Declutter

Decluttering is a process that you have to engage in for the rest of your life. You can never reach a stage in which you no longer have things to declutter. Although you might adopt a minimalist lifestyle, things get old, and you will always form new relationships.

Clutter in your life will always have an effect on you emotionally, mentally, and physically. As you create new relationships or leave old ones, there are certain possessions you have to let go of. These are constant reminders that trigger memories of these past relationships.

As you age, so also do your possessions. Some of your clothes and shoes stop fitting. You also need to change your furniture if they become unrepairable. Various things in the home often need to leave.

Not knowing when to engage in decluttering can be an issue since it promotes the development of a stress-inducing environment. You can engage in decluttering daily, monthly, or semi-annually. It all depends on you. Pick a period that you are comfortable with to take time to declutter.

Stop Complaining About Your Situation

Life is full of surprises. This is something that you must accept if you want to live a happy life. If you decide to complain non-stop about the things you don't like, it won't result in any form of noticeable change.

Stop Living Your Life to Suit the Expectations of Other People

Life can be full of stress and worries if you're always trying to please others. This is what you do when you base your life on the opinions of others. It is a people-pleasing habit you adopt to meet their expectations.

This won't make you happier. This is another ability that you develop when you finally learn to say no. You become your person.

Some situations promote this kind of lifestyle in specific individuals. This includes living with a narcissist. Everything you do will be in a bid to please this narcissist.

To the outside world, your willingness to make as many twists as you need to meet their expectations doesn't speak well of you. People hold you in high regard when you learn to say no, become assertive, and live your life according to your values.

That is a character trait that makes you attractive. If you don't already have this trait, then it is time to develop it. Say goodbye to that people-pleasing habit you have developed.

When you try to meet the expectations of others, you end up doing things that you don't like. While no one is forcing you to do these things, a part of you begins to hate those that you are trying to please. If you don't believe it, try to recall why you don't like your boss?

If they have a bad attitude, it is understandable. Regardless, there are certain people in high positions who you never interact with, but you don't like for no reason. This is because when they are around, you have to do things to please them to keep your job.

The same applies to other areas of your life. Why does a child rebel against a parent that tries to control all areas of their life?

We all like to be our person. This is a trait that is engraved deep inside us. To prevent this trait from causing you to become negative, you have to change your lifestyle.

Avoid Dwelling on the Past

Thinking about the past is often the worst thing you can do in any situation you find yourself. It brings back memories that make it difficult to move on. This is also a reason for stress in your life.

It isn't always easy to avoid dwelling. Sometimes, it seems like all you can do. In such situations, there are specific steps you can take to overcome this issue.

You can start by asking yourself a simple question. Is it worth the time you waste? This is one of the effects of dwelling on the past. You waste precious time and energy.

If you can realize that this is the result of dwelling, you can take steps to let go easily. A situation in which dwelling won't help you get the closure you need, accept what has happened, or offer a lesson isn't worth your time. Brush aside these memories.

Another step is to create time to deal with these thoughts. The inability to create time will make these thoughts linger in your mind for a long time. Although you don't pay attention to them, they remain there.

By creating time for these memories, you can face it squarely. You can do this by writing down what is bothering you and then thinking about it during the time you create. This is one way to stop yourself from losing focus when working on important tasks.

Finding the root of these memories can also help. These memories are like worries. There will be something acting as a trigger.

If you have to meet with the board of directors in a few days, then it can be a trigger for memories of your last unpleasant meeting with this same group. The way to solve it is to prepare. Your preparation involves going over your previous mistakes and coming up with solutions to prevent it from happening again.

Always having something to do is an excellent relief from memories. It occupies your mind and prevents your attention from shifting to these memories for an extended period. This doesn't solve the problem but assists in neutralizing it temporarily.

In dealing with recurring thoughts, I often tell people to look at both the positive and negative. The negative involves you carefully considering the worst-case scenario. How would you handle this worst case?

Looking at the positives involves shifting your attention to things that induce happiness in your life. Meeting up with your support group to share these things will help you forget these random thoughts.

On the idea of meeting with your support group, communication is an excellent tool in overcoming these random thoughts. Talk to people close to you about what is bothering you. Sharing your problems with others always allows you to see things from a different perspective.

If you know about mindfulness, then put it to good use here. This is a simple process in which you accept the various sensations, thoughts, and feelings going through your body. At the same time, you do your best to shift your focus to the present. It can involve doing something as simple as focusing on your breathing.

Finally, you must learn to let go. This is not as easy as it sounds, which is why I have given various steps to help you in achieving this goal.

Let Go of Your Anger

We all learn from our experiences, but the learning curve can take much longer than we often expect. This is the issue with anger. Our anger often causes a lot of damage before we learn that we are only hurting ourselves by holding on to it.

By keeping grudges and holding on to anger, you continually expend vital energy. This energy that you are regularly losing will have an effect on you both mentally and physically. It is a form of negativity that will keep flowing out of you.

Nobody wants to be around anyone that exhibits negativity. This becomes your main problem. You will end up pushing away everyone that cares about you due to your inability to let go of your anger.

What makes this more hurtful is the fact that if you don't confront the individual, you're holding grudges against, he/she won't be affected by your anger. They will go through life without a care in the world while you lose everything important to you.

Look for Ways to Make Money Through Your Passion

If you want to be happy in life, then you need money while you need to pursue your passions if you're going to fulfill your purpose in life. In my opinion, I will advise you to get greedy in your approach. Find a way your passions can earn you money.

The reason I say this is that the time you have to spend on earth can be limited. Many people often chase money to establish financial security before seeking out their passions. The problem with this approach is that you will never make enough money.

You keep working for money until you are forced to retire. At this point, there is a limit to what you can achieve due to your age and health. In the end, many people retire full of regrets.

Don't live a life you will end up regretting. Go after your passions. In doing so, apply wisdom.

Wisdom helps you understand that you need money for your survival. Don't become a liability to others in your bid to pursue your passions. If you can invest your money in ventures that offer excellent returns, then this is a suitable alternative. Be sure to consult a financial expert before making investment decisions.

Surround Yourself with People Who Care

People who don't care are usually the ones that make you unhappy about most things in life. These people don't understand you, and any form of time investment you put into such relationships will be a waste.

The people who care about you are those who know the real you and accept you despite your shortcomings. There are specific questions you must ask yourself when deciding on the right people to surround yourself with. They include the following:

- Do we share the same interests and passions?
- Will they be willing to go the same extent I will go for them?

Don't Overthink

We often have the wrong idea of overthinking. The common assumption is that it will give you an insight into your problem. You do so while seeking a better understanding.

This is far from the truth. There are several other misconceptions about overthinking and certain things that you need to change if you want to enjoy a happier life. One of these misconceptions is that the decision you take can't be reversed. This is one of the reasons why we overthink the future.

If you overthink with the belief that any decision you take now will be an accurate determinant of your future, then you are wrong. Your future is unpredictable. If decisions are the sole determinants of the future, then no one will have to struggle through life.

Although your decisions today play a significant role in how your future plays out, it isn't the sole determinant. Don't overthink because you believe there will be no opportunity to make amends. Mistakes are things that everyone has to make to live a better life.

Something that needs to change if you want to stop overthinking is your inability to forgive. This can also lead to challenges in letting go of the past. When you hold grudges, you will remain bitter most of the time.

You will also always replay the scene that led to your anger in your head. Your overthinking will become noticeable in how you continuously devise means to get your revenge.

Preparing for overthinking can also assist you in overcoming it. There are times when you are most susceptible to overthinking. These are the moments to prepare for. You can plan a family interaction during this time or try to go out for some fresh air.

What you must always keep in mind is the fact that overthinking doesn't change anything.

Changing Your Mindset

The thoughts you have regarding stress play a significant role in how it affects your life. If you want to live a happier life, you must control these thoughts. This is where a change in your mindset becomes essential.

The mindset you need when approaching your stress is one in which you see it as beneficial. If you see your stress as a beneficial part of your life, you will be forced to have positive thoughts toward it. This changes when you see it as harmful.

In this case, anytime you think of stress, you have negative thoughts. These negative thoughts also promote negativity in your life. This is what the mindset change helps you overcome.

The positive mindset gives you more motivation to face your stressors directly. You view it as an opportunity to improve yourself, improve on your existing skills, and also develop new skills. It unlocks new potential in you.

The reason why I give you the option of a mindset change is that there are specific stressors that you can't escape. The only thing you can do is to change the way you handle them. Your mindset change will give you the drive to cope successfully and adapt to the experience.

Following this change, you start to see your stress as a meaningful challenge on your journey in life. In overcoming this challenge, you get a confidence boost and a sense of pride in your accomplishment. This can be great for your mental health.

When you are faced with stress-inducing situations that promote anxiety, thinking positively will help in enhancing your performance and mood in such circumstances. Instead of stress being a barrier in your daily life, it becomes a stepping stone toward greater achievements for the day.

This is the opposite of the harmful view you often have stress. Here, fear begins to cloud your judgment, and you find it difficult to make any reasonable progress. You will start to misinterpret the anxiety that accompanies your stressor as a sign that you will fail.

What this does is to put you in an endless loop, a loop in which you develop more stress any time you face your stressors. This loop is what leads to chronic stress in your life.

The only way to overcome this is through a new attitude toward stress. How do you respond to it? How do you view it?

Depending on your answers to these questions, you may opt for unhealthy coping habits. These include resorting to smoking, drinking, or procrastinating. These will have an adverse effect on your health, both physically and mentally, in the future.

CONCLUSION

There is a lot we go through in life that makes us lose our opportunity to enjoy it—these results in what we know as stress. Learning to handle and overcome this stress is what you need for a better life.

This book will act as a catalyst in achieving this better life. It is a guide to your desires. In providing this guidance, it gives you insights into what you need to do and how to do it.

The first chapter in this book gave you a better understanding of what stress is all about, how it affects you in different aspects of your life. There was an excellent discussion on the various types of stress to help you understand that there are positive forms of stress in life.

One area that I think is significant is in the way stress affects your health. We often ignore the health implications of stress, which is why we are lax in our stress management. Knowing that it not only affects your health but also interferes with the lives of those around you can help you become more proactive.

Another excellent discussion was the introduction of the two extremes. While you have the stress-inducing situations, there are also stress control measures that you can take. Learning these control measures is a critical step in overcoming the impacts of stress in your life. If you're still having issues identifying some of the most common situations that induce stress, then I advise you go back to Chapter 2 to grasp these situations fully.

In getting you closer to your goals, there was a chapter that focused on the relationship between your stress and anger. How can you remain calm? What are the issues with anger? Does it offer any benefits? These are some of the things that you learned at the end of this chapter.

One place that has a significant impact on your stress levels is the work environment. The importance is noticeable in the fact that there is a need to keep it out of your personal life. That is to show how much of an influence it can be on your regular routines.

Your daily stress differs from your workplace stress, which is why you must come up with excellent steps in dealing with them. Overcoming stress in your everyday life requires you to develop new habits for this purpose. Your habits are things you do every day, which makes them excellent counters of stress.

Everyone loves to make lifestyle changes. One lifestyle change that people make when managing stress is to adopt minimalism. A significant benefit of this lifestyle is that in addition to stress management, it also promotes excellent money management skills. Talk about killing two birds with one stone.

A minimalist lifestyle doesn't prevent life from throwing challenges and changes at you. These are things you must deal with regardless of the lifestyle you live. Minimalism doesn't stop your loved ones from dying, and it also doesn't hinder anyone from bringing new life into the world.

You must learn to adapt and overcome these changes and challenges in life. There is no option to sit back and watch them unless you don't want to make progress any longer. Face them head-on, and you will reap bountiful benefits.

Another problem that we can't seem to escape from is worrying. When you have no escape, then the only option is to fight. This is why you must deal with your worries.

Understand how they make it into your life and learn the proper ways to handle them. If you can overcome worries in your life, then there is no chance for you to take the next step. This is preventing your work stress from getting to your home.

Worries get you to think about work, and this can be when you are supposed to be relaxing at home. This reminder can cause a change in your mood, making you irritable and less approachable by the ones that matter to you.

In the end, you must learn to live a happier life. I assist you in this by giving some of the tips I use. Happiness is free, but not everyone can attain it. How you handle your life and the steps you take will be a determinant in this.

This book promised to help you in understanding and managing your stress. From each of the chapters in this book, there was information regarding these various aspects. To ensure that it was easy to grasp, each chapter touched on a different area of stress. By combining these areas, you have a better understanding of what you need to do.

The information in this book is bountiful. Regardless, there is one thing that I always want my readers to take away. Here, I want you to grasp the concept of making money from your passions entirely.

There are several reasons why I dwell on this. The first is that your passions are the thing you love doing. You can stick with these passions for years without seeing it as a burden.

In earning money from your passions, you are doing what you love while getting what you need to sustain yourself. Working on your passions without having money will induce stress and vice versa.

Be smart in your approach. Get creative and come up with excellent opportunities to make money through your passion.

REFERENCES

Bruno, K. (2019). Stress and Depression. Retrieved 30 September 2019, from https://www.webmd.com/depression/features/stress-depression#1

Cadman, B., & Falck, S. (2018). Dopamine deficiency: Symptoms, causes, and treatment. Retrieved 30 September 2019, from https://www.medicalnewstoday.com/articles/320637.php

Gregoire, C. (2013). HuffPost is now a part of Oath. Retrieved 30 September 2019, from https://www.huffpost.com/entry/stress-aging-process_n_3047000

Kreuz, G. (2014). Chronic stress may cause premature death, new study says. Retrieved 7 October 2019, from https://wjla.com/news/health/chronic-stress-may-cause-premature-death-new-study-says-107557

Scott, E. (2019). How to Laugh in the Face of Stress. Retrieved 1 October 2019, from https://www.verywellmind.com/maintain-a-sense-of-humor-3144888

Snepp, M. (2017). HuffPost is now a part of Verizon Media. Retrieved 3 October 2019, from https://www.huffpost.com/entry/10-ways-to-reduce-stress-by-decluttering-your-life_b_58ade717e4b0d0d07e7c6654

Jennings, K. (2018). 16 Simple Ways to Relieve Stress and Anxiety. Retrieved 1 October 2019, from https://www.healthline.com/nutrition/16-ways-relieve-stress-anxiety

Purdie, J., & Sullivan, D. (2016). Diabetes and Stress: Know the Facts. Retrieved 7 October 2019, from https://www.healthline.com/health/diabetes-and-stress#types-of-stress

Rodriguez-Cayro, K. (2018). 8 Ways Even A 20-Minute Walk Can Change Your Brain. Retrieved 2 October 2019, from https://www.bustle.com/p/8-ways-walking-changes-your-brain-for-the-better-according-to-science-10077769

Whiteman, H. (2017). Chronic stress may raise obesity risk. Retrieved 30 September 2019, from https://www.medicalnewstoday.com/articles/316074.php

www.ingramcontent.com/pod-product-compliance
Lightning Source LLC
Chambersburg PA
CBHW052205090526
44583CB00015BA/1556